100 SHADES OF DECEPTION

We all have stories we don't want told!

BY CHUCK BAUER

ISBN: 978-1-09835-094-9

INTRODUCTION

THIS ISN'T THE NEXT BOOK I THOUGHT I WOULD WRITE.

I'm not a dramatic story guy, I'm a business guy. I started in sales way back in the 80s and was successful enough that people kept offering to pay me to share my expertise. I've offered in-person sales presentation training to large corporations full of salespeople. I've been invited to give keynote sales speeches across the country. People kept asking me to write a book, telling me that distilling some of my sales expertise into the printed page would help many people.

So in 2010, I wrote my first book "SalesMASTERY - The Book Your Competitors Don't Want You To Read!", published through Wiley. People loved it, which is great. But to be honest, these days sales isn't really my focus. I'd say maybe 30% of my time is still spent on covering sales, but 70% of my time is now spent teaching people about business development. I've given business development seminars all over the world, from here to Hong Kong. I have been teaching people about business for over 30 years. And for the past decade, people have been telling me, "Chuck, we loved your sales book, but you really need to write a business book!"

Well, this isn't that book. The book they're asking for is a business development book that collects some of the knowledge and experience I've gained over the past 30 years and puts it into a convenient accessible format where they can easily refer to it. And I absolutely do plan to write that book at some point. I realize that it would be a valuable reference for many of my current clients, and an invaluable resource for those who aren't able to be my clients at the moment, since it will provide many of the insights and tips previously only available to my personal clients. So you can certainly expect a business book from me in the future! I have plenty of valuable information to offer, and I want to share it.

But this book you're reading now wasn't a book I wanted to write. This was a book I HAD to write. I had to write it because the story of my relationship, the story of my life, has been told to the people in my communities from the perspective of a woman who hated me enough to betray me. The result has been that a very twisted version of this story has been going around, a story where I'm the villain and not the victim. And I need to correct the record and get my version of the story out there.

I know what you're probably thinking. "Chuck, you're not that famous, just tell the relevant people what really happened." Well, I know a lot of people. Some of them stopped talking to me once they heard the twisted version of events that made me out to be a bad guy. I tried telling a few people what really happened, but it was hard for them to accept when they didn't have the whole story. And the whole story is pretty long in the telling, as you'll see from the following 11 chapters. And frankly, I don't want to spend the rest of my life talking about this painful experience, because I'd like to move past it and just go back to being the business guy.

So here's the whole story, from the moment we first met to the day she left me and refused to speak to me ever again. I haven't spared any details, except for her name and the name of her lovers -- for legal reasons, I'll be referring to my ex as "Tootsie" throughout this book (although if you knew me over the past few years, you know exactly who she is). But all the rest of the seedy details of our relationship are in here, from the international travel to the sexual encounters with random strangers.

You'll hear about everything from the porn shop purchases to the airport sex, and how I became convinced it was my job to help my wife find other people for her to have sex with. You'll hear about secrets kept from family and friends, and the depths of deception that include an entire FAKE APARTMENT. You'll hear about a family domestic violence assault that resulted in my receiving a black eye, scratches on my face, and bruises on my shoulder from when "Tootsie" attacked me in an alcohol-induced rage, and how I still didn't raise a hand against her.

You'll hear about how I went from being a man who was having sex with a woman behind her husband's back, to the man who married that same woman and became the husband being cheated on. And you'll hear about how I should have seen some of this coming, and how my decisions helped lead me down this crazy rabbit hole of a relationship. I'm not proud of everything I did, but I have to own it, and I want you to have all the details so you can know the whole story.

Some people would prefer that you not have all these details. "Tootsie" hired an attorney and sent me an injunction letter to try to stop me from publishing this book, presumably because she really doesn't want you to hear this story. I recently learned that she has now hired a 1st Amendment attorney to sue me for the proceeds of this book, which suggests that she realizes that plenty of other people do want to hear this story, and are willing to pay for the privilege. And while I'm not willing to give her a single penny from this book contradicting her story, I am donating half of the proceeds to the Domestic Violence Hotline, a very worthwhile organization that provides help to those in need.

I know this because thanks to Tootsie physically assaulting me, I became a victim of domestic violence and ended up as someone in need of help. When I called them for assistance in my hour of need, they really kept me afloat. So I'd like to help return the favor by donating half of my proceeds to them. It's an important charity, and I truly believe they deserve the money. "Tootsie" certainly doesn't deserve it; as you're about to read, she got enough of my money already!

Anyway, that's the short version of my relationship: sex, attorneys, domestic violence, and she got too much of my money. The much longer and more interesting version follows, a full accounting of the relationship with all the scandalous details. I thank you for taking the time to read the whole story of what happened, and I promise you my next book will be about business!

--*Chuck Bauer*

CHAPTER 1:

THE SCORE AND MORE

IT ALL STARTED IN A YOGA STUDIO.

I had been going to Bikram Yoga for a few years. I had dated a gal at the beginning of the previous year, but we had broken up, and the experience had soured me on romance for the time being. I hadn't dated anyone in over a year, and I was not looking to start. I was just there doing yoga to improve myself for myself, and had no plans to meet anyone.

So I didn't think anything of it when one day after class, I came out of the studio, sat down with my big towel wrapped around me, and looked up to see a woman sitting across from me who I had never seen before. She was lovely, even though she was completely drenched in sweat. She said 'hi', I said 'hi' back, and that was the end of the interaction.

A few days later, I went to the same class at the same scheduled time, and the same thing happened again. This time she stood up, walked straight over, hip bumped me, and then sat down and introduced herself. She said her name was Tootsie and proceeded to tell me a bit about herself. I learned that she had only been doing yoga for a couple of years, lived in Dallas with her husband, and loved Italian food. She was stunning and almost dangerously charming to talk with, but she was also married, so I just chalked it up to friendliness.

4-5 days later, I was back at the yoga studio for my class, and I had arrived early. I went into the studio itself to put my mat down on the very south side and happened to notice that Tootsie was laying down on her mat on the north side of the studio. So imagine my surprise when I went out to get ready for class, and by the time I returned to the room, I saw that her mat had somehow moved from the north side of the room to the spot right next to mine.

After the class ended, she was sitting next to me and struck up a conversation. She began to tell me about her husband, who she had been married to for almost 20 years. She was not happy. She said, "He is big and fat, hardly does any work, and smokes a huge bowl of weed every night while he sits on the couch." She said that he was great at video games, but not so excellent at providing her with financial support or sexual satisfaction. In retrospect, I should have realized then what she was aiming for.

A few days later, I sent her a friend request on Facebook, which she accepted. At our next Bikram class, she seemed like she is in a bad mood, as opposed to her usual talkative self. Her husband was actually in the lobby of the studio, but he was on his phone and ignoring her. I asked her if everything was okay. She said no, but left it at that.

It's three days later that I got an early morning Facebook message from her saying she's heading to Austin on Southwest Airlines for the day, but maybe we could talk in the evening when she gets back.

It was barely 3 o'clock when I got another Facebook message from her, saying that she got done early and would like to talk. I asked her if she wanted to meet over a glass of wine. She said she'd love to, and she jumped on an earlier flight so she could come out and see me that evening. We met up at Mercy wine bar in Addison. I got us a private table, and as soon as we ordered wine, she started talking and didn't stop for about 90 minutes straight. She had a lot she needed to say, so all I did was listen.

Suddenly, she announced that she has to go. As we walked out of the wine bar, it was raining pretty heavily, so we booked it and walked at top speed to get to her car. I opened the car door for her, and when she got into the car, I reached across her to put her seatbelt on for her. As I was pulling myself back, she leaned forward and made an effort to kiss me. I was a bit taken aback, so I just said, "Have a good night," and shut the door in her face.

But this certainly did not deter her. The next week was a flurry of private messages on Facebook, and phone calls, and I have to admit there was a part of me that was a little proud and excited that a younger woman would be interested in me. (You can probably guess which part.)

A week later, she called me and asked me if I could meet her in a parking lot close to her home. I said sure, figuring that she wanted to vent again as she did at the wine bar. When I pulled up, the first thing she told me was, "As you can tell, I have done this multiple times before." It turned out that she had previously had various other boyfriends during her marriage. She told me more about her life, her disappointment in her husband's bad habits, her disgust with him being an overweight pothead slob, and how that drove her into the arms of other men. Men like me.

We just talked that night in the parking lot, but it was quickly becoming apparent that she was interested in much more than just talking. The idea of being with a married woman was new for me, but I convinced myself it wasn't an issue. She explained that she had not had a physical interaction with her husband for some time. She went on to say that she was mentally checked out of the marriage. She wanted a divorce but was afraid of actually getting one because of what her parents and family might think. I told myself this made it okay, an argument that I found especially convincing because I was very attracted to her.

A few days went by, and then one afternoon, she called me and asked if she could come over to my house. I said yes. She came over and came inside, and I said it was nice to see her and hugged her, and it probably wasn't more than a minute or two after that when the clothes came off. What can I say, we were both attracted to each other. There was nothing to stop us from having sex. And so we did, and it wasn't long until she had an orgasm, and then another, at which point it was obvious to both of us that the sexual chemistry was going to take over our lives.

From there, the relationship started to advance even though I knew I was having sex with a married woman. She spent a lot of time telling me how unhappy she was and that she had been unhappy for several years. They had tried to have kids, but it didn't work. She also told me that she had had multiple affairs with men throughout her marriage. (She did not mention any experiences with women, at this point.) But she was not being satisfied at home, so we would talk often, and occasionally she would come over for sex. Both of us enjoyed it, so the sex became more frequent.

It soon escalated to the point where we would have sex here at the house whenever she had any free time in her schedule. Like, any free time at all, even if she only had 30 minutes to spare.

For the next year, I outdid myself in trying to please her, not just with the sex, but making sure that she felt comfortable and so forth. I knew she wasn't feeling supported in any way from her marriage, so I made sure she had everything I could give her from an emotional, physical, and especially a financial standpoint.

I took very, very good care of her financially. We dined out at four to five-star restaurants regularly on my dime. Once we went into the Galleria Mall just to browse randomly, and I ended up buying her three dresses with a combined price tag of $1500. Another time we were randomly in the Galleria, she saw a $1000 necklace and said, "Oh, that's pretty." I ended up buying it for her before we left.

I should make clear that Tootsie never asked me for money or demanded that I buy expensive things for her. She never said anything about being broke or needing money. I hadn't asked about her financial stability and would have no idea how much she was earning until much later in our relationship. I just felt compelled to take care of her because I was falling in love with her. When she eventually left the house with her husband to "go live in the apartment" (more on that later), I gave her credit cards to use, just to make sure she wouldn't want for anything. And meanwhile, before she moved out, I continued to buy her expensive gifts -- gifts she was very careful to leave at my house, and not to bring back to the home she shared with her husband.

Of course, she didn't tell her husband what was going on, and unsurprisingly, she didn't tell her family either. If she wasn't even willing to talk to them about a divorce, I was pretty sure she wasn't going to tell them about an affair. But as time went on, she finally worked up the courage to tell her family that her marriage wasn't working and she wanted a divorce. She certainly did not mention me, though. I was to remain a secret.

This became trickier after she ended up filing for divorce, and needed to move out of her husband's house. By this point, she was already spending so much time at my home that she had left the majority of her personal effects here, but she still didn't want her family to know about me. She ended up renting an apartment in Addison across the street from Mary Kay Corporate Headquarters, where she worked. She deceived her entire family with this apartment by eventually having them move in her half of the furniture from the divorce. But the whole apartment was just a sham, almost like one of those cardboard cutout towns from an old cowboy movie. It was technically her apartment, but we both knew it was just a deception because for the next year, she never spent a single night there. She was always here at my house, with me.

She maintained the apartment to keep up appearances, and I was the only person to know that the whole thing was just a smoke-screen (at least until I confided in a few of my closest friends). To everyone else, the apartment was proof that she was mourning the loss of her relationship with her husband to everyone else. But the truth was precisely the opposite. We had sex every night, sometimes twice a night.

When she was getting her apartment, Mary Kay asked her to do a travel tour for events, going to Fort Lauderdale and then to Miami and then to New York City. Having gotten used to being together every night, we certainly weren't going to stop just because she had to travel for work.

So I flew into Fort Lauderdale the day after she arrived, and pretty much as soon as I got settled into my hotel room, she came over, and we had sex. We then took the Mary Kay rental car to drive from Fort Lauderdale to Miami to get to her hotel. As she was doing the Mary Kay event in that hotel in Miami, I was in her hotel room doing my online coaching sessions with my clients.

After her Miami event concluded, we went to Miami International and flew directly to LaGuardia. We were in the middle of a major snowstorm when we landed, but by that point, I didn't care. The very next day at the Marriott Marquee hotel, it was evident that I was completely falling in love with her.

I still remember that first day in New York as we were in the hotel room, I was just lying on the floor thinking what an incredibly lucky man I was, looking up at her beautiful naked figure as she put on her makeup. She was perfect. I was totally in love and completely immersed in her spirit. Life couldn't get any better than this. That moment in time was the pinnacle of the relationship.

While we were in New York, we wanted to keep up with our yoga, so we found a little Bikram yoga studio in Hell's Kitchen. And for two days, outside of her work and my work, we spent every moment together and had a great time getting to know each other at a pretty high level. She mentioned to me that she was bisexual. It was a bit of a surprise, but on the other hand, I am attracted to beautiful women, so I could hardly blame Tootsie for feeling the same way.

Tootsie told me that she would like to be with another woman, so I thought, okay, let's go to a sleazy establishment. On our last night in New York City, we decided to go to the Penthouse strip club. Being my first time at a strip club, I was anxious to see how it all worked. Tootsie never said what her prior experience, if any, had been. We were a little nervous at first, and then after a couple of drinks, we settled in.

We were in there for an hour watching everything happen, There were lots of different scantily dressed women parading themselves around. A couple of them were super drugged out but others were very attractive. There were men in suits standing around who looked like they could be in the mafia. I asked one of the suits how this all worked. He told me that you pick a candidate, and she comes over to have a drink at your table where you discuss what she is up for.

Tootsie proceeded to select a prostitute, and the discussion got very detailed as we set boundaries. I wasn't allowed to touch the girl, but I could engage with Tootsie while they were having sex. Once the boundaries were set, I paid the suit with a credit card that was authorized for additional charges if we went over the agreed time.

We went in and had a private room lined with red velvet where the two of them had sex, with me watching. It was late and we had been drinking for hours, but I will never forget how incredibly hot this was. Not only was this the first time I had ever entered a strip club, but I got a great private show.

As was to become customary (although I didn't know it at this point), after they were done having sex, I finished Tootsie off with the other girl's help. We had an early flight scheduled out, so we went back to the hotel, had some of the kinkiest sex ever, and at the height of multiple orgasms, we both fell asleep in that kinky sex position.

We were awakened at 4 am when both of our phones rang at the same time. It was American Airlines calling to tell us that we had a flight change. We were still in the same sex position that we had been in when we both passed out. Moreover, we were still somewhat intoxicated and bleary-eyed. We had a flight change and an airport change. Due to our condition, I put us in first class for the flight back to Dallas.

A few weeks later, I had a speaking engagement in Michigan, at the same time that Tootsie had a Mary Kay function in Everett, Washington. Even though Tootsie had told me before that she was not sleeping with her husband, she chose that point to tell me that he is traveling to Seattle on the back end of her trip to be with her. Talk about being caught off guard!

So I'm sitting in Lansing, Michigan, at 5:30 pm on the last day of my event, when Tootsie called me and said, "Why don't you catch a flight to Seattle? I said, "Because your husband is coming to be with you!" And she said, "Yes, I know, but you could come in for one whole day before he gets here." In retrospect, I clearly should have recognized this as a red flag. But I didn't say no. I told her I was still talking with clients.

So I finished up my meetings, and soon after she called me and said, "You have to go immediately to the Lansing airport, and then you have to change airplanes and air carriers in Chicago. I have you booked first class into Seattle. You will land at midnight, and we can spend the night together, and then at noon, you will have to leave to fly back to Dallas, because my husband is flying in right as you are flying out."

Is this not the most dysfunctional thing that you have ever heard? I agreed because I was in love with her. Again, I felt so alive with her. I am sure it's the same feeling as being addicted to drugs. In my eyes, she could do no wrong. The sex was off the chart. But clearly, so was my judgment.

I was actually at the airport when her husband's flight arrived in Seattle. Then unbeknownst to me, she spends a few more days with him in Seattle, and she was posting pictures of the two of them together at coffee shops and other photogenic venues, looking for all intents and purposes like a happily married couple. At this point, she told me they weren't sleeping in the same room. It seemed reasonably likely that they were, and I suspected she was lying to me. But somehow it didn't matter. I had to be with her.

After returning from Seattle, she accelerated the process of "moving into" the apartment (even though I knew it was just a sham). Her father and other family members helped her move out of the house she had with her husband. They put her share of the furniture from the divorce into the apartment. But as I mentioned before, she never spent even one night there, because she spent every night with me. As soon as her father drove off from the apartment, she turned around and drove right over to my home.

The relationship continued, and I started to buy her an all-new wardrobe. In addition to her clothes, I bought everything she might want in the kitchen, and I spent a lot of money facilitating all of her requests. At the time, nobody else knew that she was living here.

Once she had "moved in" to the apartment, the divorce was becoming finalized, and then Mary Kay fired her. But by that point, it didn't make any difference, because I had already been financially supporting her. The fact that her other sources of money had just disappeared was almost irrelevant.

At the end of December that first year, I realized we had been together for 11 months. We went to a Bikram Yoga retreat down in Cancun, Mexico, to celebrate New Year's Eve. We were there for five days, and we had a first-class room at the resort. That was always how I treated her, first-class everything.

On New Year's Eve, everyone who went to the retreat went to the bar, and of course, everyone was drinking – except for me. I had to keep an eye on Tootsie and make sure she was okay. She told me that there was one girl that she kind of liked who had a great ass, and that she would like to have sex with her. And she suggested that I should be the one to arrange it.

Through this whole thing, I thought that if I kept giving Tootsie everything she wanted, she would never have a reason to leave me. So, after the clock struck midnight, I approached the girl and asked her if she would be interested in having sex with Tootsie back in the room. The girl was genuinely nice and said yes, and so once the New Year's festivities calmed down, all three of us walked to the room. The two of them were drunk, and they jumped right into bed and had sex. While Tootsie was having sex with her, I had sex with Tootsie.

Just in case you have never had a threesome, let me explain. When three people are involved between the sheets, everyone is all over the place. Usually, Tootsie brought the other person to orgasm, and then the two girls traded positions or continued until Tootsie had an orgasm. I was typically behind my girl giving her pleasure. Then everybody fell asleep.

The original plan for the Yoga retreat had been to kick off the new year with 7 am yoga on the beach on New Year's Day. But clearly, that was not happening, as all three of us were fast asleep in exhausted post-coital bliss.

CHAPTER 2:

SCOTTSDALE AND WOOTSIE

SCOTTSDALE, ARIZONA. NOT EXACTLY ONE OF THE world's great centers of travel, but it was a great center of travel for Chuck Bauer, thanks to my coaching business. I had formed long-term business relationships with multiple physical fitness clubs in Scottsdale, which kept me coming back there regularly. And when I landed a significant contract years ago, I knew I would be in Scottsdale more often. It was around that time that I started to date Tootsie.

Not long after that, I had gotten a speaking engagement in Phoenix. Both of us were still caught up in the excitement of the new relationship and didn't want to spend multiple consecutive days apart, so Tootsie came with me when we flew out to Phoenix. Tootsie was by my side all the time, even meeting several of my students. She seemed to hit it off with a young woman named Wootsie, and they became fast friends.

Inevitably, I had cause to return to Scottsdale, and on our second Scottsdale jaunt, Tootsie asked me if we could meet up with Wootsie while we were there. Tootsie wanted her to join us for dinner, and then a ballet show. Wootsie seemed nice enough, and Tootsie seemed to enjoy her company, so I didn't mind.

Wootsie joined us for dinner and the ballet, and we all had a sufficiently good time that we decided to meet up with Wootsie again (outside of the business side of things where I was instructing her). It became a personal relationship where we were all just friends. Or so I thought.

Not too long after our second Phoenix trip, Tootsie came to me and asked me if we could invite Wootsie to stay with us for a weekend. This was a little surprising to me, as I didn't think they were that close. I said as much, at which point Tootsie confessed that she wanted to sleep with Wootsie.

It was still a relatively new experience for me to have a girlfriend asking me if she could have sex with another woman. But clearly, Tootsie wanted it, and by now, we both knew that I would agree to whatever she wanted. So, I invited Wootsie to come to Dallas for the weekend and paid for her ticket.

The first night Wootsie was here, we were all drinking outside around the fire pit until Tootsie went upstairs to bed. Wootsie and I were still out at the fire pit, and eventually, our conversation turned to the topic of having sex. Wootsie seemed utterly unsurprised that the weekend's escapades were to include some sex, and she walked me into the kitchen and started kissing me.

Wootsie teased me as she kissed me, "So, you invited me here because you wanted to fuck me?"

"To be honest, I invited you here because Tootsie wants to fuck you," I replied.

Her eyes widened in shock, and she immediately stopped kissing me, literally threw her clothes off, and then ran up the stairs to jump in bed with Tootsie.

I followed Wootsie up the stairs at a more measured pace, and by the time I walked into the bedroom, the two of them had already started having sex. After they finished, Tootsie asked me to finish her off. I was only too happy to oblige. The rest of that weekend was spent shopping and enjoying other expensive entertainment. We might have gone to another ballet performance; I cannot recall. All I remember is that our jobs for the rest of the weekend had now been carved out. I was the one continuing to spend money, and the two of them continued to have sex. Little did I know then, Wootsie would have a much larger role to play in our eventual divorce.

Over the next couple of years, there were various times where we went to Scottsdale, or when Wootsie came here, and we continued having threesomes together. Not only was there a lot of sex, but a lot of vibrators and porn. I regret many things about my time with these women, but I must admit there was a lot of pretty extreme incredible sex. Most of the time I facilitated, doing different positions and using sex toys with the two of them. Tootsie had probably $4000 worth of sex toys and sex furniture, and Wootsie became the beneficiary of that, and of me helping them along. Suffice it to say, there were lots of orgasms.

We fell into a rhythm and would get together for threesomes once every three months. Typically, it would start with the two of them kissing, and then they would finger each other, which would inevitably lead to the two of them in the 69 position. When that was going on, they would either want my cock or the vibrator. The one that got them off the quickest and the most was a double dildo with a vibrator attached. A lot of times, Tootsie would have me position Wootsie a certain way. It is all kind of hard to describe, but it was mutually satisfying over-the-top sex. It was beautiful, in a way.

Wootsie became a fixture in our lives, even joining us on numerous trips to Napa. And the sex was constant. The only time I can recall that the three of us went on a trip and *didn't* have sex, was when Tootsie and I eventually got married in Grand Cayman. There were only a few close family members and Wootsie there with us. But that is a story for another chapter.

Another thing that was weird when that all three of us were sleeping together, Tootsie would wake up every morning, come over to my side of the bed, and have sex with me while Wootsie was asleep. Tootsie and I had sex EVERY MORNING, and she kept this up even with Wootsie right next to us soundly sleeping! As soon as Wootsie was here for a weekend, like clockwork, Tootsie would wake up and want to have sex with me, with Wootsie fast asleep right next to us. I think maybe it was her way of reminding me that she was Number 1.

CHAPTER 3:

PROMISCUOUS AND FOOTSIE

ABOUT 6-7 MONTHS INTO OUR RELATIONSHIP, TOOTSIE mentioned that she has had a long-running affair with a guy named Footsie. At the time, I was shocked. In retrospect, I probably shouldn't have been, given that I knew she was unhappy with her ex-husband (and obviously our relationship was proof that she wasn't going to settle for loneliness in a loveless marriage). But at the time, I was very flustered and demanded more details.

She told me that Footsie was married with two children and that he was a corporate executive at Susan G Komen while Tootsie worked there. That is when they started their long-time running relationship. She continued to see him after she left and started at Mary Kay. And when she says she continued to see him, she means physically.

But the strangest twist to the whole affair may be that Footsie's wife ended up working for Tootsie as her housemaid. I realize I can't cast any stones about dating someone married behind their spouse's back, but you have to admit, it's a whole other level to do that and then make their spouse clean up after you. And Tootsie's relationship with Footsie went on for many, many years.

He and his family were invited to Tootsie's parents' home every year for the annual shrimp boil festival that they hosted. This was a big party with typically 30-50 people, so it didn't seem strange that Tootsie's friend Footsie was invited. But that's because nobody knew that they were sleeping together. Her parents didn't know, her husband certainly didn't know, and Footsie's family didn't know.

She went on to tell me that she and Footsie shared an apartment in Washington, D.C., for several years. I just found the whole thing strange, because back when we had first started dating, she had told me that the reason she hadn't gotten a divorce was that she was so worried about her reputation. But then she revealed to me that she has had all these things going on for years, which, in my mind, would be a lot more scandalous than a divorce. Go figure.

Regardless, the thing with Footsie turned into this long-time relationship with them sharing an apartment in Washington, D.C., since he represents a Dallas Medical Facility as a lobbyist. She told me this affair had been ongoing for years.

Then she informed me that at one point, she had a pregnancy scare with him. It did not occur to her to use sufficient protection and birth control in all her fooling around, so there was a brief period where she worried that she was pregnant with his child. It is one thing to be so hungry for sex that you go around having sex with random people, including guys who are already married. But to risk pregnancy is a whole other level of irresponsible. What would she have done if she had gotten pregnant? She would just be there at her family parties, pregnant with Footsie's baby, while his wife continued to clean up as the housemaid. It would probably push her to get an abortion.

And then what would have happened if she had the kid? Would Footsie have acknowledged it, thus being forced to reveal the affair to his wife? What would it have done to Footsie's marriage? And if he did not want to acknowledge it, but she told his wife, the likely outcome would be destroying Footsie's marriage and making things very tense between Tootsie and Footsie.

A pregnancy scare with your girlfriend in a normal situation is challenging enough. But facing the possibility of pregnancy when you are having an affair with a married man is an entirely different level of problem. I think she was very irresponsible, and it is clear to me that if she had ended up being pregnant, that could have ruined some people's lives.

Luckily, that turned out not to be the case, and she never became pregnant with Footsie's child. Or maybe not so luckily; it's likely that if she had become pregnant with his kid, I never would have started dating her, and I could have saved myself many heartaches and no small amount of money. It would have been an obvious sign to me right up front of how many people she was sleeping with, and the amount of care she was taking (not enough).

But of course, that did not happen. The pregnancy scare turned out to be just that – only a scare – and Tootsie was not responsible for another human life. And a good thing too, since it seemed like she could barely even handle being accountable for her own. After this whole pregnancy scare episode, you would think she'd have learned the dangers of what she was doing, and the severe risks of having sex with a married man. Perhaps she took her near-disastrous experience to heart as a lesson in why it is essential to be more careful?

Not at all. As far as I can tell, she learned absolutely nothing from the entire experience, and it did not stop her from continuing to see Footsie, despite the possible consequences. Worst of all, she told me that since she had been living here, she had not only kept in communication with him but had seen him "once or twice."

At this point, I got upset. I spoke with a little anger and a little hurt in my voice and said, "Tootsie, you can't tell me you are in love with me, and then still keep seeing your boyfriend over the last ten years!" So, she promised me that she was going to break it off. She said she would go meet with Footsie and two other guys in her fantasy football league, and at the end of the meeting, she will break it off with Footsie. She went to that meeting, and then came back and reported that she had broken it off with him.

I did not believe her. Looking back, I don't think that her meeting even included these other football team guys. I am sure it was only with Footsie. And I am sure she did not break things off with him then. Hell, I bet if you did some digging, you'd probably find that she's still currently with him as I write this. I do not know that for sure. All I know for sure is that during that period of time when Tootsie was fucking him behind everyone's back, his wife was still serving as Tootsie's housemaid. Footsie always brought his wife and children to the shrimp boil with Tootsie and her family.

That may be the extramarital hookup of Tootsie's that stood out for me the most, over the years, but it was only one of many. I continued to learn just how many as our conversations grew more intimate, and she became more comfortable in confiding in me.

At the time, it barely even phased me. I was still high on the supply of love, and between our intimate conversations and the wild-ass sex every day, I was convinced that our relationship would last forever no matter what. When Tootsie revealed to me her desire for other women, I didn't view it as a threat, because she was still having sex with me. And I felt like I was contributing to Tootsie by encouraging her, or sometimes agreeing to keep an eye out for opportunities for her. At times, it was almost like I was her pimp, except that I was also the one paying.

This is how stupid I was: I thought that if I could help her satisfy all of her sexual needs and desires, it would further our relationship. But I did not realize just how far all of her sexual needs and desires extended.

And the more we talked, the more I learned. During some of my intimate communication with Tootsie, she would show me texts on her phone, revealing how she really viewed relationships. I was just too dumb at the time to understand what it meant.

Her longest-running group texts were a group of four of her best friends who had all grown up together. They would regularly be sending texts and pictures to each other about every random thing, from texts about college gossip to pictures of pets and lunches and holiday vacations. But among that group of best friends was Tootsie's best friend, Anne.

Anne is a college professor here in Texas and had a separate private text chat running with Tootsie which was not shared with the rest of the group. It was easy to understand why once Tootsie showed me what they were constantly texting back and forth about -- a series of boasts comparing their conquests of male partners. It almost seemed like they were in some sort of sex competition with one another. And Anne was having a lot of one night stands, so Tootsie seemed eager to have enough wild sex to top her.

The two of them also rated the men that they slept with, assigning a number from 1-10 to rate how good the sex was. Whenever Anne texted that she had fucked a 10, she would put the number 10 in a ridiculously large cartoon font, and Tootsie would text back, "You go, girl!" Tootsie would also text Anne ratings for her own male conquests. I was far from the only one on the list; I'm just glad to have rated a 10.

At one point, Tootsie had shown me one of her texts where Anne was bragging about having sex with "two 5s at the same time" where she had said to Tootsie, "That counts as a 10, right?" I was surprised that these were the kinds of private conversations that women had with one another. I don't even talk like this to my male friends.

But I shouldn't have been surprised. During that period, we were watching a lot of porn together. Tootsie has her favorite female porn actresses, Jillian Janson and Kimmy Granger. And 90% of the time, she wanted to watch those two porn stars.

We must have bought half of the videos these actresses ever made. There were a lot of them, all paid for by me, of course. There were videos of the porn starlets doing a lot of solo exhibitionism, lewd acts with other women, and threesomes. Tootsie seemed to be most interested in the threesomes. It's possible that a single person could never satisfy her sexually. But the more porn we watched, the more she got the idea that she wanted to be with multiple people at once.

Naturally, I did everything I could to make her desires come true. Even though she was the one who wanted this, I took charge of the process of finding her people to have sex with, in hopes that doing so would show her I could give her everything she wanted. I started searching for couples or women who wanted to have a lesbian encounter on Craigslist.

And Craigslist is not like Amazon; you can't just do a search, read a review, and then order the product and be reasonably sure you're getting what you wanted. On Craigslist, there is a lot of crazy sex shit going on there, and there are zero verified reviews, so it's a lot of effort to separate the wheat from the chaff, or shaft.

I would do some serious vetting of people before inviting them into my home to have sex with my wife. I would communicate with people and figure out whether they were worthy, asking questions and trying to sort out what kind of people they were. In addition to trying to figure out if they were people I could trust, I also had to figure out if they were people Tootsie would want to fuck.

I finally found one couple that seemed responsible and friendly and not crazy -- a rare find on Craigslist. They lived out of Murphy, which is not too far away. So, on a Friday night, we ended up meeting them in Addison for dinner, to chat in person and see if we still wanted to give them the green light. We had a pleasant conversation over dinner, and they seemed like a lovely couple that had their stuff together, with no giant red flags of drama or emotional issues. However, the woman's photos had to be from at least ten years ago. She had aged and put on a few pounds from the pictures she had sent.

Still, I decided that I trusted them, and then Tootsie gave me the signal that she was interested, so I invited the couple over to our house with us. At the time, this was a very new situation for us. This was not a situation like Wootsie where we had someone we both already knew and liked, and then decided to make things sexual. This was a completely different set of circumstances, and we didn't know a lot about how this all went on. It was like a lifestyle for some people where it was a frequent and regular part of their lives. Whereas for Tootsie and me, we knew it would not be frequent or regular but would happen every once in a while as Tootsie needed to satisfy her sexual urges.

This was still kind of weird for us because we were completely new to the whole thing, so in the car on the way home from the restaurant, Tootsie was asking lots of questions about how everything worked. And I didn't know yet, so we had to negotiate it once we were there.

We all came back to the house and talked about having sex and what the ground rules were. The girls had a strong sexual interest in each other. But the husband said that he wasn't interested in having sex; he just wanted to be a casual observer. I was also not allowed to have sex with the other man's wife. Not that I was interested anyway, as I thought Tootsie was much better-looking. Then, Tootsie said, "Okay, but when she and I get done having sex with each other, can I fuck Chuck?" They said yes.

So, all four of us went upstairs, and the girls proceeded to take off their clothes. With their clothes off, it was even more obvious that the other man's wife was not as attractive as Tootsie, not even close. But Tootsie was interested in her, and so here we were. I also took my clothes off and sat in a chair to watch. The other man sat on the other side of the bed and left his clothes on. I am not sure if he could get it up to begin with, which may be why he didn't want to participate.

The girls' interaction probably lasted 30-45 minutes and involved multiple positions as well as some vibrators. They both had at least one orgasm. Tootsie probably had multiple. As they started to slow down, Tootsie asked me to take care of her. I proceeded to start having sex with Tootsie, and at the same time, I asked the woman to do Tootsie's clit while I was fucking Tootsie, and she was also grabbing her breast. Tootsie had another massive orgasm. I also came.

After I got done, everyone got dressed, and we came downstairs. They said, "We would like to be in touch with you again," and then they left. The next day, I got a text from the husband that just said, "Thank you for a fun evening." The day after that, he sent another much longer text, explaining that his wife wanted Tootsie's cell number so the two of them could develop a relationship and become friends.

It was pretty clear that he meant his wife wanted to be the kind of friends that also have sex frequently. When I told Tootsie and showed her the text, she made a very sour face and said, "No. No way. I don't want to be friends with them, and I don't think I even want to have sex with them ever again." So that was the end of our relationship with that couple.

I don't know if it was regret on Tootsie's part, but you have to remember she was already having sex with Wootsie. Even if you ignore the fact that Wootsie was much more attractive (a point tough to ignore when you are having sex with people and seeing them naked), sex with Wootsie was an utterly over-the-top experience, so I think Tootsie's bar was set very high.

Regardless, that experience didn't satisfy her craving for multiple sex partners at once, especially given that the husband didn't participate at all. So, back to Craigslist I went, to investigate more possibilities. A few days later, I came across this thing that said, "Four hands massage". So I called the guy, who was up in Plano, and he explained that he and his wife would do a double team on one or two people. This sounded like exactly the type of thing that Tootsie was looking for. But again, it's Craigslist, so I had to exercise due diligence.

I vetted him for probably two whole months, over the course of which I would have an occasional conversation with him and ask him to send pictures of himself and his wife. And they seemed like they were kind of just ordinary people, not unattractive but not particularly attractive either. They just seemed like regular people, not wild and crazy sex maniacs. But I suppose that to the rest of the world, Tootsie and I probably just looked like ordinary people too.

Once I had satisfied myself that this couple was safe for us to interact with, I told Tootsie about the whole "Four hands massage" thing and asked her if she wanted to do it. She said yes. So we set it up and arrived at these people's apartment in Plano. They had obviously been doing this for a while because they were very discreet, and there was a system they had set up for getting there and paying them and everything.

Yes, we paid for the massage. It might seem strange to pay for Tootsie to have sex with strangers from Craigslist, given that so many people were perfectly happy to have sex with her for free. Before I married Tootsie, it would not have occurred to me to go on Craigslist and pay for sex. Although at least there you pay up front. I certainly ended up paying for my sex with Tootsie in the long run!

But meanwhile, our exploration of random Craigslist couples looking for free sex had not gone as well as I'd hoped, so I thought maybe by paying people, I'd get better results. And while I don't know if I'd call these people professionals per se, clearly they had done this before and been paid for it, and they had systems in place, so I hoped that it would be the type of experience Tootsie was looking for.

As Tootsie and I already agreed, she would take off her clothes and get on the massage table, and I was merely going to watch. To kick off the experience, the man and his wife took off their clothes.

The wife ended up naked, while the man kept his boxers on. They proceed to do a "Four hands massage" on Tootsie. What that entails is both of them doing various sexual things to Tootsie, grabbing, squeezing, and penetrating her.

And amidst all of that, this is the part that I found strange: Tootsie was very quiet. Typically, whenever Tootsie is out doing sexual things with people, she is very vocal. Moaning, groaning, squealing, yelling, "Give me more," that kind of thing. I have plenty of bad things to say about her, but nobody ever accused Tootsie of being silent in bed.

Yet here she was being worked over by two people at once, which I thought was what she wanted, and she just seemed reticent. So, at the end of that hour, she finally said, "Okay, that was great, thank you." And that's it, four hands massage was over. The couple put their clothes back on, Tootsie took a shower in their bathroom and put her clothes back on, and then we left. In the car on the way home, she said she did have an orgasm at one point, but she thought the whole experience was just "okay," and had no interest in doing it again.

Which was fine by me. This wasn't something I had been excited about doing because I had any interest in four hands massage from Craigslist; I had simply tried to help Tootsie satisfy her sexual urges any way I could. I thought as long as I could keep meeting all of her needs and desires in whatever way possible, it would further our relationship and make it stronger. And for some time, it seemed like it was working. The more that Wootsie became active with her sexually, I thought, the better it was for me.

In the long run, that turned out not to be true. Tootsie continued to enjoy the sex they were having together and stayed intimate with Wootsie, but did not stay intimate with me. She never told me

TRULY what was going on with her. And this after I had done every-thing I possibly could for her. My sexual appetite was all about her. I had trawled Craigslist for couples because that's what she wanted. And when that couple came over to my house, I didn't even want to screw the wife, I just wanted to screw Tootsie afterward. So I felt like I had been as nice a guy as you could ask for, respectful enough of her desires to let her have her thing so she could have orgasms and multiple orgasms, but cared enough about her pleasure that I always took my turn with her afterward.

Indeed, our sex with Wootsie was proof that my focus was clearly on Tootsie's pleasure. With Wootsie, we had sex a lot; we saw each other every 6-8 weeks, and basically what I did was facilitate vibra-tors for them. Whenever we got together, the sex was initially just them. Then I would finish both of them off, and only then would it turn into all three of us together in various interchangeable positions. For example, Wootsie would be on her back, I would be inside of her, and Tootsie's clit would be on Wootsie's face, all while Tootsie would be kissing me and holding me. Then the roles would be reversed.

Wootsie was a regular part of our lives. When we traveled to Phoenix, we were so comfortable together that Wootsie would just stay with us in our hotel room. Our schedule was pretty much the same every day. In the afternoons, I'd take care of all the online coaching I had to do, while Wootsie and Tootsie toured around town. In the evenings, we'd go out to dinner at an upscale restaurant, and then take in a show. After the show, we'd stop at a wine bar and have a few drinks. We would then go back to the hotel room and end up screwing all night long until we all fell asleep in the same bed. And we would wake up in the morning together and then do the whole thing over again day after day until it was time to fly home.

So it's not as if Tootsie ever lacked for sexual excitement. She had her various irregular flings, our regular relationship with Wootsie, and the two of us were continuing to have sex daily. In addition to all of this, there were probably 2-3 instances each week where we fired up one of those porn videos with her two favorite porn stars for Tootsie to live out her fantasies.

For someone who was having sex with his wife instead of hiring prostitutes, I ended up spending an excessive amount of money on sex. The pile of porn videos did not come cheap. And neither did Tootsie. She came quite expensively; I probably spent over $5,000 on sex toys when I was with her. And that's including the 10% discount I got at the porn shop for being such a frequent customer. After a few years with Tootsie, I knew every single person who worked at the porn shop.

One time we went into the shop to buy Tootsie another sex toy, and we noticed a cute girl at the counter we hadn't seen before. "You must be new," said Tootsie, as she was ringing us up.

"Yeah, I just started last week," said the girl. "I guess you come here pretty often?"

Tootsie smiled. "I come pretty often. I like sex. Hey, if you like sex too, perhaps you'd be interested in joining us for a threesome?"

I saw the girl's face light up as she raised her eyebrows in surprise, but then after a couple of seconds, she sighed. "You're beautiful, and I totally would, but I know my boyfriend would disapprove."

"Your loss," I said, as we walked out with our new sex toy. It was a shame; the girl was very cute.

Still, Tootsie and I continued to have an incredible sex life. At times it seemed like our relationship revolved around sex. I think it became most evident to me when we put mirrors in the bedrooms, and I realized we had become the kind of people who put mirrors in their bedrooms. And I was okay with that. I wanted to put a mirror on the ceiling, and for whatever reason, Tootsie said no. But we both liked to watch ourselves while we were having sex.

So we did end up putting mirrors in the bedroom. There is one tall mirror on one side of the bed upstairs, probably 5 ft tall and 2 ft wide. On the other side is the same size mirror, just hung horizontally instead of vertically. And somehow the mirrors managed to magnify the experience of the sex. We are both very visual people, and so with the mirrors, it seemed like there were four people there instead of just the two of us. We both liked to look at all aspects of ourselves having sex and somehow having sex while seeing ourselves in those giant mirrors added to the experience. It was pretty incredible, in a way that's hard to describe.

I think you can tell a lot about a relationship from the architecture you build in the bedroom. If you see a couple with giant mirrors in their bedroom, this is a couple that's probably having a lot of sex. So mirrors are a good sign.

Fortresses, not so much. One time as we were lying in bed after having sex, Tootsie told me about her ex-husband. She said she sometimes slept in the other room and sometimes slept in the same bed with him. But whenever she slept with him in the same bed, she said she made a "fortress" around herself from blankets and pillows to make sure he couldn't touch her even accidentally in their sleep, because the very thought of him repulsed her. She didn't love him anymore and was just there until she could set herself up with someone better.

One night a couple of years later, towards the end of our relationship, I noticed that she had pulled all the pillows and blankets in our bed around herself. And I found myself thinking back to this conversation we had shared, and wondered if she still loved me.

Looking back, my guess is probably not. It was around then that she started getting a lot of late-night texts, and I'd be willing to bet that they were from some other guy that she already had on the hook. I think she probably had six weeks of planning to leave before she even said anything.

I began to wonder if Tootsie always knew that she didn't want to be with me for the long haul. There was a particular phenomenon that I could never explain, but whenever Tootsie, Wootsie, and I were at a public venue, she became almost a different person. Whether it was a ballet, or a bar, or just a random outdoor gathering, she would always treat me very differently than she did at home when it was just the two of us or just the three of us.

All three of us would be at an event together enjoying ourselves, and then like clockwork, Tootsie would suddenly just walk off until she was 20-30 yards away. She didn't seem to have any particular destination, she wasn't walking to a refreshment tent or the bathroom, hadn't been waving at a friend or heard anyone calling her name, she would just up and disappear for no apparent reason. And she never offered a reason or even an acknowledgment that she was doing this, never any "Hey, I'm gonna go over there for a minute," never any, "Come with me," no indication whatsoever that she was aware of the other people that she was with.

And I had no idea what she was aiming for. Maybe she was trying to get away to meet up with someone else she was having sex with? But she never got too far away to see, so it doesn't make sense that she'd be meeting up with anyone else. Maybe she wanted to check her phone for messages from someone else she was seeing? But she wouldn't need to walk away for that, since she was constantly checking her phone while we were all standing together, and I rarely saw who she was texting.

Maybe she expected that I'd follow her? If that's what she wanted, I don't know why she wouldn't just tell me, unless it was some weird sort of power trip to see if I would follow her around. And let's be honest, at that point I was so completely invested in giving her whatever she wanted, that if I knew that was what she was hoping for, I probably would have followed her around all night.

But I didn't know if she wanted me to follow or just walked off because she wanted some space, so I didn't want to intrude by following her around. Instead, I was just left standing there with Wootsie, as we tried to figure out the mystery of what was going on. Sometimes, I think Wootsie was even more dismayed than I was, as neither of us had a clue as to what Tootsie was up to.

I wondered if Tootsie was using our public outings to try to scout for someone "better", and didn't want to be seen with me. Although she was very affectionate at home, when we were in public she wouldn't even hold my hand. It was like she didn't want the world at large to see us as a couple, or see her as unavailable. In spite of all the wonderful things I had done for her, whenever we were out in public, she would ignore me and just walk off in random directions.

There were some times the three of us were out at an event that Tootsie was so rude to me that I just had to leave. I would get to the point where I couldn't take it anymore, would grab a cab, and just leave. I just can't figure out why she was so rude and inconsiderate.

We did have a 20-odd year age difference, so it's possible that it was just a generational thing. My parents taught me good manners and proper etiquette, and I went to cotillion and everything to make sure that I knew how to treat people considerately. It was pretty clear that social graces were not high on Tootsie's priority list.

But then I remembered that Wootsie was right there with me, and although Wootsie was pretty close to Tootsie's age, she somehow managed not to be close to Tootsie's rudeness. All three of us had been at a number of these events, and while Tootsie would constantly walk off without so much giving us a wave, Wootsie never did anything like that. After the many times as Tootsie was rude to me, sometimes to the point where I couldn't bear to continue the evening and just went home, Wootsie never did anything like that. So maybe it wasn't a generational thing, and maybe Tootsie is just a rude person.

Towards the end of our relationship, in the last 6-7 months of our marriage, she started getting phone calls and text messages into all hours of the night. Part of that may have been business-related, but I could also tell her attitude had changed because of the late-night texting and communication. In retrospect, I realize that our relationship had come full circle. We first met because I was the more interesting attractive man she would rather talk to (and fuck) than the husband she didn't love, and by the end of things I had become the husband she didn't love, and I suspect she was up all night talking to another man she was more interested in.

As I look back, I know that I made many mistakes. And I am genuinely sorry for what I did – or in some cases, did not do – over the course of our relationship. In all my years and the various adventures I've had, traveling all over, my relationship with Tootsie was just the craziest story that I have ever had anything to do with.

CHAPTER 4:

TRAVEL FAR & WIDE ON CHUCK BUCKS!

OF COURSE, BACK WHEN WE WERE STILL IN THE FIRST years of dating, I had no idea of all the unpleasantness awaiting me at the end of our relationship. I was in love and was convinced that I could easily solve whatever small problems might arise. Tootsie was still officially living with her husband but had already moved in with me, so I knew it was just a matter of time before she finally got divorced and we could build our life together.

But we were not quite there yet. And I could tell that Tootsie was not yet envisioning the same perfect, stress-free life together that I was. It was during this time that she was fired from Mary Kay. Tootsie panicked because she was not divorced yet, which meant she was still dealing with all the fears related to her current marriage. She was afraid that her parents would find out that she was living with me and had lost her job. And she was especially worried that she was going to run out of money. Her husband at the time did not earn enough to support their household without her income as well. She said he made about 20K a year, and without her money from Mary Kay, she knew this would not be enough for the two of them.

To me, this was an easy problem to solve because all it needed was money. Of life's various problems, I have always said that the ones you can solve with money are easy; the other kind is more complicated. (This would turn out to be especially true about our relationship.) But meanwhile, I calmed her fears by telling her she did not need to worry about the money, because I would take care of her. I loved this woman, so I wanted to protect her. And I knew I could afford it, so if I could make her life better without making my life too much worse, it seemed like an obvious decision.

Looking back, though, I see that she took advantage of my offer. I intended to provide her with a safety net, so she didn't have to worry about going broke and would know her needs would be taken care of until she got back on her feet with new employment. Instead of looking for another job, she was out of work for 18 months. I continued to work and pay for everything for both of us. She was living off of Chuck Bucks, and I'm sure to her it seemed like an endless supply (probably because she didn't have to go out and earn it). I think she enjoyed just having everything taken care of, and had decided that if I was willing to pay for everything, there was no reason she needed to rush back to finding a job and having to show up at an office.

The biggest thing that I want to convey is that I took her pretty much all over the world, experiencing the best of everything, and she never paid for any of it. I think perhaps in her mind, she was paying me with sex. But the Chuck Bucks were paying for all the bills, and the bills got very expensive. Over two-thirds of the trips we went on, she was in first class. And on the rare trips that we flew in coach, we were always able to get massive legroom on the Airbus A321.

Because I own a business development consulting company, I can take my work on the road with me, making it easy for me to travel and work from anywhere. And sometimes, I am asked to travel for work to meet with clients on-site or to speak at conferences, not only in the United States but also internationally. So travel was a constant thing for us.

In the five years we were dating, we traveled to far more places than most people will see in a lifetime. Of course, the place we frequented most was Scottsdale, Arizona, at first because I had a lot of business there, but later also to see Wootsie. We went to Tucson in Arizona as well, to take advantage of the scenery and the wineries. And we went to Phoenix eight or nine times, mainly to see Wootsie. We'd stay at a 5-star Hyatt, with the three of us all in one room. These Phoenix jaunts lasted three or four days, so we were able to spend lots of time together.

On what turned out to be the final one of these trips together, Tootsie asked me on the last day of the trip if we could move to Phoenix. I wasn't overly interested in the idea, as I felt like Phoenix was a nice place to visit, but I preferred living in Texas. She asked me again later that same day if we could move to Phoenix since it would be more convenient for seeing Wootsie without needing to hop on a plane. Again, I said no.

In retrospect, I wonder if that was the primary precursor to Tootsie's explosion, and her eventual decision to abandon me entirely. I had denied her constant contact with Wootsie, and I suspect that she may already have been more interested in spending time with Wootsie than she was in spending time with me.

Of course, our travels extended far beyond Arizona. We went to all the most exciting places in the country, and even when I was there on business, we always made time to see the sights.

We went to Austin, which, although it's technically still in Texas, almost felt like a different state from Addison. Austin is renowned for being a little weird, but we mainly enjoyed the live music and good sushi. Of course, when it comes to regional food, it's hard to beat New Mexico. We often went to Albuquerque, where the roasted chiles make everything better -- which I needed because that was also where we would visit her family.

We went to Detroit a few times when I had to for work, although admittedly, we ended up spending the bulk of our non-working time in the hotel. Raleigh, in North Carolina, was somewhere I often had to travel to speak at conferences, but there we were more likely to poke around town to take in a ballet or hit the nature preserves. Portland, Oregon, was another place where we took in some waterfalls and made time to appreciate the great outdoors and wineries.

In other places we traveled, it seemed like the thing to appreciate was the great indoors, which was undoubtedly the case in Las Vegas. It was easy to spend endless hours just wandering the casinos, and of course, the big shows provided a spectacle that Tootsie enjoyed. We often experienced Cirque du Soleil, although Elton John was the most enjoyable show that we saw, for my money (and it was all my money).

We went to Vegas multiple times with Wootsie, where the three of us would get an oversized suite. Vegas is a very sex-focused town. The shows all have scantily clad women soft-selling sex. And of course, if you knew where to look, there were plenty of people hard-selling sex as well. We'd spend the days in our luxurious suite having threesomes all day long, and then go out to see entertainment at night. Everyone else also appeared to be thinking about sex, as evidenced by the fact that Tootsie must have been hit on 15-20 times. Wootsie received her fair share of attention as well. Vegas with two hot women was undoubtedly an exciting experience.

We frequently visited California, from the beaches of San Diego to the wineries in Napa Valley. We must have gone to Napa together at least four times, usually bringing Wootsie along as well. The girls loved visiting the wineries there, and who wouldn't? I'm sure it helped that all the wine was on my tab. Throughout all our Napa trips, I probably spent $20,000 on wine for the three of us, which was a lot more than the $2,000 per year I had spent on wine before marrying Tootsie.

Still, it's not as if I didn't get my money's worth on those Napa trips. We got to meander through the beautiful vineyards, drink a variety of the world's best wines, and just soak in the days.

We'd occasionally hit the East Coast as well. We went to Orlando, where we spent the obligatory day at the theme parks. I think Tootsie would have been happy to live at Disneyworld. Still, I figured since we were in Florida, we should take advantage of the ocean, so I convinced her that renting jet-skis would be a better use of our Saturday. After an hour on the water, I think she agreed with me.

I may have already mentioned the Ft. Lauderdale escapade we shared back when Tootsie and I had started dating. Tootsie was there for business and met me at my hotel so we could have sex. We then rented a car and drove to Miami, where we stayed at a hotel I'd spoken at, and had more sex. And then we flew to New York City, where we ended up getting snowed in for a delightful evening. I ran my meetings virtually, we went out to numerous restaurants and strip bars, talked about bringing prostitutes back to the room, and had lots of sex until we passed out.

On subsequent trips to New York City, we left the hotel room a little more often to take advantage of the non-sex-related sights that NYC had to offer. We saw the Statue of Liberty and Times Square, and I let Tootsie visit some of the high-end Fifth Avenue shops where I treated her to a lovely dress from Saks and a gorgeous necklace from Tiffany's. All the shopping, dining, and hotels were completely covered for her, courtesy of Chuck Bucks.

I never asked Tootsie to pay her way, nor did I expect her to. I no longer even expected her to find another job. As long as we were a couple, I knew I could support her until she got out of her lousy marriage funk. She did help me pack for my travels and was very good at making sure I had everything. I appreciated her company and the extra things. And she ALWAYS remembered the sex lube.

Once we were going through security at DFW, and one of the agents rummaging through my suitcase pulled out a small plastic bag with a sex lube. The agent held it up high and said, "Sir, you can't have this." In a LOUD voice, I said, "Hell, that is sex lube, and we use that quite frequently, could you please let it pass this time?" The agent began to crack a smile and looked a little embarrassed. "Sure," she said, as she stuffed it back in the bag with a big smile on her face, "have a good time!"

I can only imagine what that agent would have thought if she knew what we got up to at other airports. Between all my travel for business, and all the vacations I took with Tootsie, I must have racked up a gazillion miles with American Airlines. This qualified me for all their premium perks, including Admirals Club membership.

So whenever I flew, I'd specifically try to use airports that had an Admirals Club.

Admirals Clubs let you rent rooms with showers. This is a definite plus if you're traveling a lot for business and need to freshen up before an event. But it's also convenient for other reasons. Whenever we flew to Grand Cayman, we'd always have a layover in Miami, where they had an Admirals Club. We'd rent ourselves a room, and since Tootsie and I were heading out to a sex-filled vacation and were stuck in an airport with nothing else to do, we decided to get a head start on our vacation sex. It really put the "lay" in "layover".

Having sex at the airport became a routine for us. In addition to stopping into the Miami Admirals Club every time we were en route to Grand Cayman, we'd rent a room there whenever we were in Miami, even if we were just there for a Mary Kay event. We frequently used the Admirals Club in San Francisco as well, as well as various others at larger cities across the world on occasion. Most Admirals Clubs had mirrors in their bathrooms, so that added to the sexual pleasure of the experience.

Eventually, we got so accustomed to having sex at the airport that it became a necessary part of our travel arrangements. We'd pretty much always end up renting a room at whatever airport had an Admirals Club and have sex to break up the tedium of the flight. And if the airport didn't have an Admirals Club, that didn't stop us. We found that the handicapped bathroom was very rarely used at many airports, and was surprisingly spacious. At Phoenix airport, among others, Tootsie and I would have sex in the handicapped bathroom. Yes, I became one of those people who have sex in airport bathrooms. I'm not proud of it, but it happened.

All of that was going through my mind as the Dallas Fort Worth security agent found herself slightly embarrassed by my sex lube. "Lady," I thought, "You don't know the half of it!"

In addition to all of our travels around the country, we traveled internationally as well. We often visited Canada, going to Toronto, Montreal, and Vancouver multiple times. We always stayed at 5-star hotels with huge baths and regularly visited the city's finest restaurants. Vancouver is somewhere I used to go back when I was single, and I recall the city being fabulously beautiful mid-summer, always bustling with activity.

I took Tootsie to Vancouver twice, once when we had ten days off and were looking for a perfect extended getaway. Vancouver was as beautiful as I remembered and surprisingly clean for such a large city. We explored the area, biking all over and hiking up an 8,000-step elevation mountain. When our feet were too tired to move any more, we saw the city while riding through it on open-air buses.

Of course, Tootsie was rarely on a trip where she wasn't also thinking about sex. Before our big Vancouver trip, she had asked me if I could find her a sex partner in Vancouver. And I did my best, by way of a lot of advanced Internet searching, but came up empty and couldn't find anyone suitable. Nonetheless, at our 5-star Renaissance hotel on the waterfront, Tootsie managed to find someone she decided was suitable – a hostess working at the hotel.

Over the course of the week we were staying there, Tootsie fell head over heels for this woman that she had barely talked to. As you might expect from a hostess at a 5-star hotel, the woman was attractive, but as usual, Tootsie didn't want to talk to the woman herself, so she asked me to convey her interest and set up a sexual encounter for her. Ever dutiful, I did what Tootsie asked and approached the hostess to ask if she might be interested in a sexual encounter with Tootsie, but the hostess politely declined. This came as a grave disappointment to Tootsie.

Still, I'd say Vancouver was one of our favorite destinations out of all the vacations Tootsie and I took together. Both times I took her to Vancouver, she pitched a fit as we were leaving, because she was so disappointed to have to come back home to Texas. She asked if we could move there, and while I wasn't ready to give up my life in Texas, I did give serious consideration to the idea of summering in Vancouver. I thought it would be nice to spend three or four warm months there every year, maybe volunteer at a farm and work with animals. Most of my work is online, and Tootsie wasn't working, so nothing was standing in our way of spending summers wherever we wanted.

I was thinking about doing this, but we didn't manage to work out the details before Tootsie decided to abandon me for no reason. It was a shame because I would have given her pretty much anything she wanted, including summers in Vancouver if that's where she decided she wanted to spend her time. I already was giving her more than most people ever dream of receiving, between all the luxurious vacations, the gifts, and of course, arranging for her to have sex with other people. But I guess somehow it still wasn't enough.

Kamloops was another one of our Canadian vacations, where we spent a week at a horse ranch. We had been thinking of an entertaining vacation that we'd never taken before and hit upon the idea of a dude ranch. The two of us sat in my backyard, on dueling laptops, scouring the Internet to see who could find the best dude ranch vacation. We looked everywhere from Colorado to New Mexico, but the best-sounding place was in Kamloops, British Columbia.

So we planned a week-long vacation there, flew out to Vancouver, took a smaller plane to Kamloops, and then drove 45 miles up 7,000 feet to this fabulous dude ranch where everyone was very sensitive to how they worked with the horses. The guy who owned the property was a chef and would cook for us, we had great wine, and the trip was mostly fantastic.

The exception was our last day of the trip when Tootsie and I went out for a ride along with two of the ranch hands (who were both girls). As we rode, we saw a big herd of cows, probably 500 head, and got to watch the cowboys wrangling them, which was always a fascinating thing to watch. They went down the road, and about an hour later, we followed the same path on horses.

We stopped when we came up to a cattle guard, and then we saw some of the other cowboys riding in on horseback with some Blue Heelers by their side. (Blue Heelers are cattle dogs especially well-suited to working as herders.) Unfortunately, one of the Blue Heelers did something that spooked our horses. I didn't see what it was, because one minute we were all calmly sitting there on our horses staring at the cowboys, and then suddenly, all four of our horses turned, reared up, and began galloping away as fast as they could run.

If you have never been on a horse when it gets frightened enough to bolt into a full gallop, you can count yourself lucky. We're used to horses because we've trained them, but the fact remains that these are massive, powerful beasts. In this case, I was on an enormous horse, the largest one out of the four being ridden by our party because I'm 6'3", so they had given me the big horse. So when my giant horse began running full gallop, I got bucked off and was nearly killed. I felt lucky to have avoided a severe injury.

One of the cowhands was not as lucky; she also got bucked off her horse, but then the horse came down and broke her ankle. Not great, but still could have been worse. The other cowhand had managed to stop her horse without getting bucked off at all, a testament to her skill. Tootsie was likewise able to stop her horse, although it helped that she had been given the smallest horse as the smallest member of our party.

When I got back to Dallas after that trip, I blacked out a few times, wracked by the injury. But despite that last ride with all the problems from the spooked horses, it was a phenomenal trip. It's still so weird that Tootsie and I enjoyed all these beautiful vacations together. We saw the best that Canada had to offer.

We even honeymooned in Montreal, with four-star reservations at the Renaissance Hotel. We ended up getting food poisoning because we went to Quebec City, but that's a story for another time. Old Montreal was beautiful, a quaint little city with an old area just like Paris. Tootsie went as far as hiring our Cayman wedding photographer to take pictures of us in Old Montreal – I realize that may sound extravagant. Still, the images were incredible, to the point where I felt like we could have been on the cover of a modeling magazine. Admittedly part of that was due to Tootsie's beauty, although I'm in pretty decent shape myself. Still, the photos themselves were just fabulous, and I felt like we had captured magazine-worthy images that would live on FOREVER.

I don't know how Tootsie just turned around and walked away from all that. Maybe nobody will ever know because she'll never tell. Or maybe she just fell more in love with Wootsie than she was with me, and decided that what she loved most was the freedom to have multiple affairs. I'd be willing to bet that she was having numerous experiences while we were married without my knowing, especially since she was doing so after. And somehow in her mind, that was more valuable than a lifetime of incredible vacations with someone who would pay for all of it because he wanted to take care of her.

The most significant trip we ever went on was a ten-day trip to Hong Kong. We flew there in business class, and her ticket round trip was still $5,500, of course, paid with Chuck Bucks! Hong Kong was amazing, almost like a whole different world. I think it's the only place we traveled where English wasn't the predominant language, although thankfully, most of the people we had to interact with did speak it. But it was strange to be surrounded by a massive city of people all speaking a different language. This was especially true in the giant street markets, where endless stalls offered every kind of shopping you could imagine. But unlike New York City, all the shops here were open to negotiations, so the streets were loud with the sound of customers haggling with the shopkeepers, mostly in Chinese. The whole trip was unique, and I'd recommend it to anyone looking to get away and experience something truly different.

We went to Cancun, which is technically in Mexico, but specifically the Mexican Caribbean, and it feels a lot more like the Caribbean than Mexico. Endless coastline as far as the eye can see, white-sand beaches, and stunning ocean views that you could spend hours just staring out at -- and we certainly did. Seeing Tootsie in her bikini only added to the view. And, of course, Tootsie had a girl fling while we were in Cancun!

I think of all the places we traveled, Tootsie's favorite was Grand Cayman. Between the beautiful beaches and the fine dining, I don't think there was a place on earth that she enjoyed more. We must have gone there together at least half a dozen times throughout our relationship. We even had our wedding there, which I'll talk more about in the next chapter.

But across all of our travels, across the US and abroad, from New York City and Orlando to Hong Kong to Cancun, the one constant factor is that everything was paid with Chuck Bucks. They covered the entirety of our travel, not only paying for the entire trip itself but every possible thing Tootsie could want while we were on vacation. I spared no expense was spared at hotels, restaurants, or any of the places she wanted to shop. She was treated to the best the world had to offer, and I paid for all of it. I surrounded her with luxury, and it never occurred to me that I was just setting myself up.

And why would it? As far as I was concerned, I was proving that I would take care of my woman and always give her the best. What woman wouldn't want that? I certainly had no way of knowing that she would suddenly turn on me a few years down the line. I just knew that she enjoyed travel, I wanted to travel with her, and I was in a position to give her more of what she enjoyed. And there was no place that she enjoyed more than Grand Cayman.

CHAPTER 5:

GRAND CAYMAN

I HAVE A GOOD WORKING RELATIONSHIP WITH MULTIple clients in the Caymans who are great people. For a few years, I was teaching a business consulting course in Cayman every six months. I had a nice footprint there, with very prominent and successful clients as well as other less prominent people and businesses in the Caymans. There are two types of people who were my Cayman clients: The ones who were wealthy, and those who were beyond wealthy. I have done a lot to increase these people's companies, which is why they keep asking me back.

After Tootsie and I started dating, not only did she want to join me in the Caymans, but she wanted to take scuba lessons. I provided that for her, of course. One exciting thing about the Caymans was that while nobody in the United States knew about our relationship, we didn't feel a need to keep it secret in the Caymans. We were able to enjoy ourselves and not hide the fact that we were dating. Everyone says what happens in Vegas stays in Vegas, but corporations have known for years to go to the Caymans if you want a haven.

So I flew her to Cayman numerous times, and she met some elite wealthy people. She was showered with gifts, beautiful sunset dinners, and sunset cruises on luxurious boats. She got caught up in the lifestyle and loved being in the Caymans. It became our go-to vacation spot. She would run up $1,200-$1,500 bar tabs per day, which included getting the most expensive food on the menu and buying drinks for other people that we met. Or people she hadn't met yet but wanted to.

One of these people Tootsie wanted to get to know better was a hostess she had noticed at the Westin, who she thought was very attractive. The hostess was sweet and had significantly large breasts. We ended up inviting said hostess to meet us at the Ritz one night for drinks. We met at the bar at the Ritz, and as I'm sure will come as no surprise, we ended up back at our hotel room having sex. We were all drunk, and again Tootsie, after finishing having sex with the hostess, asked me to have sex with her. She was insatiable.

After numerous trips to the Caymans and many other travel adventures, including Vancouver, Toronto, the Okinawa Valley in British Columbia, and various other destinations we traveled to because of my work, we began to feel like it was time we got married. She was accompanying me everywhere. Yet, her family still didn't have a clue that any of this was going on. We had been to the Caymans together at least three times, and her parents never even knew I existed because they thought that Tootsie was still in mourning for her prior marriage.

But Tootsie had an elaborate plan to slowly introduce me and cover up the fact that she had been lying to everyone for a year and a half. In retrospect, I should have recognized the ease with which Tootsie could cover up her consistent lying for the warning sign that it was. Her divorce finalized, and then after a certain amount of time, she went to her parents and said that she had met a new guy (me) and that we were dating. Keep in mind, she had already been living with that "new guy" for 18 months.

We had already been talking about getting married, and now that her parents finally knew about me, we talked it over and thought, yes, it's time. Her parents had probably six months of getting to know me, after which Tootsie finally revealed to them that she was living with me. I'm sure her parents thought it was reasonably fast for her to move in with someone she had just started dating a couple of months ago and then already be thinking about marriage. If only they knew.

Her parents came to the house and blessed the relationship. I thought about it, and I asked Tootsie if there was a particular kind of ring she would like for the engagement. She told me about one that she had once seen long ago in New York City. It was two diamonds, sandwiching a ruby in the middle. I couldn't quite picture it from her description, so she gave me a picture. It looked like a very atypical but beautiful ring, and I resolved to buy it for our engagement. Yet, in the back of my mind, I thought this is the ring that she picked out with her friend, Footsie!

Unfortunately, it was more difficult than I had expected. I spent about two months trying to buy that ring, but things did not work out, and I couldn't find another one anywhere. At this point, I was kind of at my wit's end. She had her heart set on that specific ring, and I had made it my mission to be sure that I could give her everything she desired. I knew I couldn't kick off our marriage by failing to get her the ring she wanted.

So, I ended up calling Wootsie in Scottsdale and asked her for help in getting a wedding ring for Tootsie. Wootsie pointed me to a local jeweler in Scottsdale who does custom jewelry, so I could have a conversation with him about building Tootsie the perfect ring that she has in mind. After going back and forth over details, I contracted with the jeweler to create the exact ring that Tootsie wanted. It came out to be $27,000. Future enhancements to that ring took the total price up to $34,000!

It took a lot of work and effort to get that ring, both to find a place to buy it, and then to pay for it. I had to buy the ring with a down payment and then get it financed, so I'd be paying for it for a year. But I needed the ring soon because I was trying to plan the engagement around Thanksgiving when I knew that Tootsie's family would be in town. As always, I was doing everything for her, nothing for me.

So, late in 2017 with Thanksgiving rapidly approaching, I came up with an elaborate plan. I would bring Tootsie to a private yoga session with one of our favorite instructors, Ainsley. In addition to teaching yoga to us that day, Ainsley would also be in on the caper. The secret plan was that Tootsie and I would be in Ainsley's yoga studio, where unbeknownst to

Tootsie, we had hidden the ring was under the edge of my mat. I knew I wanted to surprise Tootsie with the proposal and figured the middle of a yoga session would be when she would least expect it.

Everything went as planned. A few days before Thanksgiving, Tootsie and I showed up at the studio, where Ainsley proceeded to take us through an advanced course. About 50 minutes into the class, we're doing an acro yoga posture where I'm on my back and holding Tootsie up with one hand, and she is looking straight down at me. I reached my other hand behind me underneath the mat, grabbed the ring, pulled it up, and put it right under her nose. She started hyperventilating and crying and completely freaking out.

Somewhere amidst all the tears and burbling, she did manage to say, "Yes, I will marry you!"

Cleverly, I had my staff waiting on standby. And a friend of mine who is a great photographer came in to capture the moment, and my assistant came in with champagne and hors d'oeuvre, and we had ourselves a little party. I have to say, that was probably one of the top moments of my life. It wasn't cheap, but it was a glorious time.

Due to Tootsie's love of the beautiful white sandy beaches of Grand Cayman, and the convenient lack of people down the road (since we didn't want any random people spoiling our perfect day), we chose that spot to get married. We planned the wedding for February 24th, which gave us about a 4-month engagement period. Tootsie handled the engagement announcement, and of course, between her PR background and her natural tendency towards taking things to the extreme, she went hog wild. She must have sent out hundreds of announcements with our picture, gushing over how happy we were. We told everyone we were having a private wedding in Grand Cayman with only family and a few best friends.

The wedding was beautiful, really one of the most picturesque locations in the entire world. There were just miles of breathtaking sandy beach, and nobody there to spoil it. Our families were there, as were a few close friends, and of course, Wootsie. Even as we were getting ready for the ceremony, my best friend Joe asked me, "Why is Wootsie here?" He didn't know about our threesomes. I just told him that she and Tootsie had become closer friends, which was technically correct.

It had rained all morning, and it kept raining all day, right up until the time we were to be married. And then the clouds broke open, and a ray of sun beamed down onto the beach. It was a truly magical moment.

One of my Cayman clients, an ordained minister, married us in a short and sweet ceremony. After the ceremony was complete, we took some spectacular pictures.

We hired a bus to drive everyone around so everyone could be together since we had kept the whole thing to barely two dozen people. We all piled into the bus to head out to dinner at one of the island's top restaurants located right on the water's edge. Arriving at the LUCA restaurant, the sun was going down and just about to dip below the horizon. I grabbed Tootsie, and we ran with the photographer to the edge of the beach, and that photographer captured one of the most beautiful pictures of a couple ever on the beach.

We then headed back to the restaurant, where about 20 of our closest friends and family were waiting for us. We had a great meal with great wine and great friends, and it was one of the most spectacular moments of my life. We ran up about a $5,000 tab and had ourselves a great little wedding meal. I think that our engagement and wedding were probably the two high points of our relationship and my life. Everything was simply perfect, and I figured I'd found happiness at last.

4-5 months later, Tootsie and I decided to go back to the Caymans. We rented a Cabana at the Westin, which is directly adjacent to the Ritz. One of my favorite funny responses to anyone who says I'm too much of a spendthrift with my constant jet setting around the Caymans is to tell them, "Hey, I'm frugal; if I wasn't frugal, I would stay at the Ritz!"

I like the Westin cabana because we get additional service and attention and can bring up to 12 guests to enjoy the 5-star service. On this occasion, we had invited some very dear friends of mine: Marty and Wendy, who I have known for 40+ years. Marty is a physician, and Wendy is a small business owner, so we had met them at the cabana on this beautiful summer day.

Marty and I decided to walk on the beach, leaving Tootsie and Wendy at the cabana. Wendy told Tootsie that she was going back to her hotel room and would be back in a minute. Wendy went up to her room but left behind her beach bag, in which she was carrying $700 in cash. I should mention that it is not uncommon for Grand Cayman people to have that kind of money with them. Wendy goes back to her room and returns 20 minutes later to get her bag and head to the beach. Marty and I returned from our walk. As far as I knew at the time, nothing worth mentioning happened on that day.

Only a year and a half later, when Wendy found out that Tootsie had physically assaulted me and filed for divorce, did I suddenly learn the true story of that day. That day Wendy had $700 cash stolen out of her beach bag and spoke to hotel security to see if they had any leads. They reviewed their camera footage of the common area, and in one of the frames, it showed Tootsie looking in Wendy's beach bag. It was difficult to see what happened because one end of the beach bag was blocking the camera. But given that nobody else was on camera messing with the beach bag, Wendy strongly suspected that Tootsie had taken that money. But because I was so happy with my new wife, and had been kind enough to invite them out to the cabana, Wendy didn't feel like she wanted to risk a rift in our friendship over $700 and had kept quiet. Kept quiet, that is, until I had already become aware of Tootsie's more destructive nature and wouldn't be upset at an accusation of thievery, at which point Wendy filled me in on the details.

The whole thing still bothers me to this day. I don't understand why Tootsie would feel like she had to steal money when I provided everything for her. $700 wouldn't have even paid for a single day of the vacation I was giving her. I can only conclude that she was essentially intent on making as much money off of me as she possibly could, over the whole course of the relationship. And again, it's not like she needed money while she was with me. I paid for everything she could want throughout the entire relationship, and she never had to spend a penny.

CHAPTER 6:
TOOTSIE'S FAMILY

NONE OF US JUST APPEAR IN THE WORLD FULLY FORMED. We are all, inevitably, influenced by our families, both through genetics and our environment. Sometimes you can learn a lot about a person by meeting their family or understanding their relationship with their family.

My case is no exception. When I was 14, my parents divorced. Less than a year later, my mother committed suicide just a few days after my 15th birthday. My father was so devastated that he retreated into his own head and never fully engaged with the world again. So there I was at 15 years old, Mom had killed herself, Dad had checked out, and I needed to take care of myself because nobody else was going to. I went to four different schools in the next nine months and had to learn to support myself financially before I even got my driver's license. I knew I had to take full responsibility for my own life because I couldn't rely on anyone else. Did this factor into how and why I became an independent businessman and entrepreneur? Gee, you think?

Tootsie's family was very different and much larger in the number and size of the members. The most obvious difference was that her parents were still alive. Tootsie was in constant communication with her parents and regularly had gatherings with members of her family.

Both of Tootsie's parents came from large families. Her mom's family was from Minnesota, and her Dad was from Socorro, New Mexico. It was hotdish meets taco bowl, two cultures that placed a lot of importance on family. It was very different from what I had grown up with. Her family seemed almost like the Godfather, where the families would intervene and talk to each other about big decisions.

So I learned early on that any decision that Tootsie made, her family was probably involved somehow. In a way, I admired that, as it was a kind of support that I never really had. However, Tootsie was a trained Public Relations expert. I saw this trend of her manipulating information. It was her job to SPIN the outbound communication for Susan G. Komen, Mary Kay, and the American Heart Association. However, her expertise in spinning also carried over to our personal lives. It was tough for her to be authentic! Not only with me, her husband, but also with her family.

As I overheard her conversations with different family members throughout our relationship, I noticed that the ways she communicated to her mother versus her father or brother were all very different. She would tell them each a different version of the same story, customized for her audience at the time. She called this "controlling the narrative." My internal nickname for her became "The Spin Doctor." I would later realize that this was Tootsie's way of maintaining control over everything, and everyone, in her sphere. But I was flush with love, so I saw things in a different light at the time. I had just started to notice patterns, and said to myself, "Hey, this spin doctor skill she has from work, she applies it at home too. That's interesting." All seemed benign until I was the one who ended up getting spun.

I have 30 years of being in business, and those 30 years taught me a lot. Those suspicions I had about Tootsie's spin-doctoring were spot on, but I ignored my instincts and did not react to them because I was so in love with her at the time, I thought she could do no wrong. And this was despite the obvious evidence to the contrary. I very clearly knew even then that she was controlling and never 100% truthful. The best example is that she lived in my house for over a year, and her family had absolutely no idea. She had put her talents at deceiving people to constant, well-practiced use, but I didn't see any malice in it until it ended up hurting me. I know the difference between right and wrong, but I don't think that Tootsie did. She was convinced by her deception as well. A self-trained narcissist! A wolf in a sheep's body!

But while Tootsie's spin-doctoring would eventually ensure that her family looked on me with disfavor, the first rift in my relationship with her family came about because of a conversation I had with Tootsie's aunt and uncle. We had flown into Albuquerque to visit them.

I told them the story of this when I first moved into my house in Carrollton, Texas. I had come home from doing a seminar and pulled everything out of my car so that I could put everything away. Some items stayed in the garage, and some went into the home. I had a few books, huge stacks of papers, my laptop, and a $2500 projector for the presentation I had given. This projector was top of the line, Optoma with HD resolution, the works.

I had placed the projector and a few of my books right inside the garage (door open), grabbed my laptop in one hand, and the huge stacks of papers and such with the other hand, and brought them into my house. I remember looking down the street, and I saw a black kid walking down the road. When I put the laptop and papers down inside, I walked right back out to get the projector and books. The books were there, but the projector was gone. I called the Carrollton PD and filed a police report, but the projector was never found, nor the one suspect that I thought probably did it (or for that matter, any other suspects).

So the uncle said to me, "Well, isn't that a little racist?" I said, "No, it's not racist. I'm just saying exactly what I saw. A black kid was walking right by my home with an open garage door and a very expensive projector in plain view. It stands to reason he probably did it." Tootsie's uncle took offense to that and called me a racist. I wasn't having any of that. I categorically denied being a racist and told him not to call me one. We were sitting at his bar, and he got out of his chair like he was going to hit me. Tootsies' aunt had to get in front of him, so he didn't assault me. I think he doesn't like me because he is Hispanic, and some of his family members are on welfare. So, I think he saw me as an evil white man because I own my own business and am very successful. Something that Tootsie benefited immensely from, by the way.

So that was how I got off on the wrong foot with Tootsie's uncle. And it wasn't the only time, either. Once, when I was speaking with her uncle, he asked me questions about how he could improve his business. I gave him the same answers that I have given to hundreds of other people, and once again, he accused me of being racist and told me I shouldn't use those tactics. I'll give you an example.

One of the issues he was having was with staffing. He told me that he was having a hard time hiring the right people for his company and keeping good people working for his company. He asked me to give him a few tips about hiring better people and retaining them. This is something I often get asked, as a business coach, and my answers are always the same:

My number one hiring tip is finding people who already have DISCIPLINE built into their personality. Finding them is easy – you recruit people who have prior careers in the military, boy scouts, and virtually any athletes. Those people usually have a great deal of discipline and are used to carrying out orders and directives. How simple is that?

My number two hiring tip is to REQUIRE forty-five-second video cover letters from all applicants. No video, no interview. It is that simple.

And, saving the best for last is: Do a Full Car Check on the Applicant. During the interview, you ask them about the car that they drove to the interview; you ask the make and model and wherein the parking lot is it parked. You physically walk outside and do a walk-around-inspection of their car. You look inside the vehicle, checking to see how the inside looks. This will be a reflection of how their office or desk area will look! If their car is CLEAN and not littered with trash, their desk will typically be the same.

This is called a "third-level" appraisal. The third level means that we get BELOW the waterline to see what the applicant is genuinely all about. In the sinking of the Titanic, the iceberg was only thirty feet tall above the waterline. The iceberg UNDER the water went down 300 feet.

Tootsie's uncle was taken aback because many of the poor people in New Mexico drive un-washed and unclean cars.

I have given these tips to hundreds of coaching clients, but it was evident that after these conversations with Tootsie's uncle, he began to hold me in contempt. And not just him, but his entire side of the family. And this was a side of the family that had initially liked me when they met me. Because of these different views, I fell out of favor, and it started to create a rift between Tootsie and me. I am sure the whole family was talking about me among themselves. As Tootsie would put it, they were using "back channels." And I know that their opinion had a strong influence over Tootsie.

It's not as if that side of the family didn't already have plenty of drama to deal with. You may recall, back when Brett Kavanaugh was up for the Supreme Court, and they had a big hearing in front of Congress to vote on whether or not to confirm him. Tensions were heightened worldwide because of this, as the accusations of sexual harassment and sexual assault came to light. As the hearings were winding down and Kavanaugh was appointed, a breaking news bulletin came from Tootsie's mom's side of the family. It was another sexual misconduct allegation, but this time, much closer to home: Two of Tootsie's aunts had come forward and accused Tootsie's father of raping them.

This sent shockwaves through the family, as you might expect. According to her aunts, one of them had been raped two decades ago, while the other occurrence was just a year and a half prior. And where the two sides of the family had all been very close in the past, this created a severe rift in the family, as everyone was forced to choose between believing Tootsie's father or believing Tootsie's aunts.

From my standpoint, it was hard to believe that such a thing would happen because Tootsie's father was not only a man of small stature but also a very kind and gentle man I had enjoyed getting to know. But at the same time, you had two women accusing him of rape, and one not being a distant childhood memory, but only 18 months prior. There were records in two different police departments of these rape accusations.

Tootsie and I were married at this time and knew of the situation, but I didn't know all the details of precisely what was going on. And part of this was by design, which I would later learn was a direct result of Tootsie's controlling nature. Tootsie had eagerly jumped into the middle of the public relations nightmare with both feet and started to control everything. She mostly wanted to maintain control of all communication. She got her family new phones so they couldn't talk to anyone that Tootsie hadn't explicitly approved. All communications for the entire family suddenly had to go through Tootsie.

And she wouldn't let her parents email, talk, or do anything with anyone, because she didn't want them to make a mistake and let slip a single word or quote that might be used against them. At this point, everything had to go through an attorney. And her parents were exceedingly afraid that word would get out about the alleged rapes because Tootsie's father is also a very prominent figure in Boy Scouts of America. So Tootsie ended up in control of all communications for her entire family. The spin doctor could spin everything as she liked.

I should mention that I supported Tootsie's dad fully throughout all of this. I counseled him and consoled him because I always thought he seemed like a good guy and had a hard time believing he would do anything like what he was accused of. And you'd think that kind of support during a very trying time would have endeared me to him and put him on my side forever. But blood is thicker than water, as they say, and when Tootsie and I eventually had our falling out, he wouldn't even talk to me. His daughter assaulted me and came very close to getting arrested (more on that later), and when I begged him to help me arrange a conversation with Tootsie to talk things out, all he said was that there was nothing that he could do.

Despite all that, looking back on it, I enjoyed Tootsie's big family and being included in it for a while. I grew up in a very different environment, and my family is few and far between. With my parents' divorce and mother's suicide both looming large in my childhood, the family environment that Tootsie had grown up with seemed like a whole different world to me. I can see now how my lack of close family figures in childhood increased my desire to be included in Tootsie's seemingly perfect family life.

Of course, no family is perfect in reality. Her uncle thought I was a racist. Her aunts thought I was supporting a rapist. And naturally, Tootsie was in the middle of it all controlling all the information as usual, giving different stories to different people and only telling everyone what she wanted them to know.

So perhaps it shouldn't surprise me that even when Tootsie ended up violently assaulting me and ending our relationship, her family still saw her as someone who could do no wrong. And why wouldn't they? She almost certainly had told them her version of the story in which she was the innocent victim, and I was the bad guy. And she was their family, so they weren't going to give me a chance to tell my side of the story. As far as they were concerned, Tootsie was someone who could do no wrong.

But I knew better. And you're about to know better too.

CHAPTER 7:
THE YOGA COMMUNITY

AS I'VE MENTIONED MANY TIMES THROUGHOUT THIS book, Tootsie had an absolutely insatiable desire for sex with other people. No matter how much sex we had, how much porn we watched, it was never enough for her. And when Tootsie told me that she wanted to have sex with other people, I decided I didn't have to worry as long as she was still with me. She was still having sex with me, and we still did other things together, like yoga. But I don't think I realized that what I saw as a yoga community, she saw as a yoga community and sexual buffet.

In retrospect, I wonder how many people she was approaching at our yoga studio before we started dating. After all, our relationship had started because she pretty much showed up out of nowhere and threw herself at me, moving her yoga mat to be next to mine. She was aggressively showing interest and trying to kiss me early on, and pretty much relentlessly pursuing me until we ended up having sex. Could I have been the first person she ever acted like this with? Somehow, I doubt it.

More likely than not, she had been hitting on random people in our yoga community long before she and I had gotten together. She had a whole studio filled with people she could quickly evaluate based on physical fitness, as she got to see them stretching and sweating without too many clothes on. And as a young and attractive woman herself, I'm sure she was able to find willing participants.

And if she had approached people in our yoga community for sex before we started dating, there's no reason to think that she ever stopped once we started dating. Even before we had gotten to the point where she felt comfortable asking me to take part in her attempts to set up sexual encounters, she was often non-present towards the beginning of our relationship, and I strongly suspect that she was using the yoga community as a place to groom people and seek out sex.

My primary evidence for all this is what she did after we had dated for a while. The only difference was that now when she wanted to explore sex with other people, she often roped me into approaching people because I was a better communicator than she was. But even early on in our relationship, she would often be gone for an extended period where I didn't know what she was doing, and she'd occasionally mention that she had gone on a date with someone else from the studio.

Literally within the first month of my dating Tootsie, our studio had been visited by a Bikram yoga teacher who worked directly for Bikram himself. He had come to teach here in Dallas, and the surprising thing about him is that he was quite overweight, which is very abnormal for a yoga teacher. Many of the students at our studio agreed this was very strange, as Bikram yoga teachers are generally very thin, so this guy was a complete anomaly.

Despite this, Tootsie told me that she had gone on a date with this guy. Now technically speaking, I don't know if it went any further than just one date. Still, knowing how much Tootsie loves sex and thinking about how often a very overweight man has the good fortune to be propositioned by an attractive young woman, I imagined that it ended up being more than just a date.

At least that one was all Tootsie. It wasn't long before she had involved me in her yoga community conquests. As usual, I played along willingly because I knew it was what she wanted. I had reasoned that logically speaking if I helped her satisfy all of her sexual needs and desires, I'd be providing her with the perfect relationship that she'd never had any reason to leave. But I just hadn't counted on how far all of her sexual needs and desires extended. As she began to push me to help set her up for sexual encounters with other people in our yoga community, I was soon to find out.

Prior to our wedding, a national competitor had come to teach at our studio. You might think it's strange for competitive yoga even to exist since yoga is supposed to be all about the mind-body connection and generally is one of the least competitive activities you could imagine. Still, in the past decade, competitive yoga has actually become a real thing in the US. This woman had made it to the national level of competition, so you know she had considerable skill.

She also had an attractive figure, and Tootsie expressed some interest in her, asking me in my role as the "Great Communicator" to invite this woman to join us for dinner and a show. I did just that, and the woman accepted, joining us for a nice dinner out, followed up by a very entertaining show. As spirits were high, I took the opportunity to pop the question and ask the woman if she might have any sexual interest in Tootsie. But the woman said no, and so that was the end of that.

Another time, there was a practicing student at our yoga studio who was very fit. Tootsie had, of course, noticed her first and pointed her out to me, wondering if I might proposition her on Tootsie's behalf. I thought the woman was charming as well, and since we were both interested in her, we decided to invite her out on a date. The evening went swimmingly. We all had a lot of fun and were talking up a storm over dinner. I thought there was a lot of chemistry and was pretty sure this student was going to show some interest in coming back to our place after dinner to fool around, but then it ended up being Tootsie herself who decided against it at the end of dinner. She signaled me that she was no longer interested in inviting this woman over to our house after dinner, and so it didn't happen that time either.

This is not to say that all Tootsie's attempts to hook up within the yoga community met with failure. She indeed found willing participants now and again. One instructor had come to the studio a while after we married, and this woman was every stereotype of the incredibly strange hippie yoga teacher that you could imagine. She talked in a weird way, had some very odd beliefs, and even gave herself multiple names, none of which were normal. Around the studio, the name she used most often was "Persephone."

Anyway, Tootsie went to lunch with this woman and informed me that her lunch date had turned into a lunch and sex date. And apparently Tootsie enjoyed it, because she told me that she wanted us to try to set up a threesome with her. We made two attempts at it, but it never worked out – which is honestly just as well, because I think that gal was crazy.

I'm pretty sure there were other yoga community conquests as well, but those are the ones that Tootsie told me about. I have no doubt there were plenty of others I do not know of because Tootsie's sexual appetites were insatiable. Indeed, our time together showed me that she had no self-restraint when it came to looking for sex from anyone and everyone at our yoga studio.

I wonder if part of the reason was our yoga community seemed to believe her word over mine when it came to the facts of our divorce is that she had slept with some of them. I was shocked at the time since this was a community of people I had thought were my friends, and after my breakup with Tootsie, it seemed like almost all of them took her side, even though she was lying -- and I have evidence to prove it. But if she was sleeping with some of them, that would certainly help explain why they decided to believe her and ignore everything I was trying to tell them.

Everyone was just lovely to both of us in the meantime since we were still together. Nobody had to pick sides, because it seemed like Chuck and Tootsie were inseparable. At least, until August.

CHAPTER 8:
THE BEGINNING OF THE END – AUGUST 2019

AS I'VE MENTIONED MANY TIMES THROUGHOUT THIS book, Tootsie was always a very controlling person. She wanted to control information, decisions, and especially people. Whenever she wasn't in control, she felt powerless and found it maddening. This is probably why she always had such an internal fire to dive into analytics in her business life and to overanalyze everything in her personal life. She needed to have all the information to have all the control, to have all the power.

I used to tell people that Tootsie would sacrifice happiness to tell other people that she was right, and that she would rather be correct and in control than be happy. But in retrospect, I think the truth may have been more stark: She couldn't be satisfied unless she was in control and felt that she was right. And for most of our relationship, I never noticed it because it never came up. She always thought she was right, and I gave her everything she asked for (and plenty of things she didn't even ask for), so for all intents and purposes, she was in control, and I never argued with her.

In 2019, that started to change. During that year, I began to see a fundamental change with Tootsie, and I'm not sure if it was caused by other things going on in her life or just the fact that it was the first time we ever disagreed on anything. I suspect that she had other things going on behind my back because our disagreements certainly didn't seem severe enough to explain her reactions. But on the other hand, it was one of our first real disagreements.

My business had started to accelerate, and I was paying down debt and becoming nearly debt-free. (I will note here that if not for all the money I had spent on Tootsie, between the wedding and the ring and the vacations and sexual escapades and gifts, I would have already been debt-free by that point.) She got into an argument with me about the three outstanding loans I had yet to discharge, all of which were nearly paid off. Those were our house, a second mortgage on the home for a remodel, and our Cadillac Escalade.

All three loans were within a point and a half of each other. So it's not like I was balancing a 19% APR credit card debt against a 6% mortgage debt. All three of them had roughly the same interest rate, so it wasn't that big of a deal which one got paid first. Tootsie got into a significant disagreement with me about which loan to pay off. She had overanalyzed all the numbers (of course) and concluded that she wanted the car to be paid off first, and then the second mortgage, and then lastly, the house itself. I told her that the percentages were so close that the financial difference barely registered, and I wanted the personal accomplishment of saying that the house was free and clear. Anyone who has ever paid off their home knows the tremendous feeling of satisfaction you get from achieving that, and that's certainly worth a few dollars at half a percentage point more on some other loan.

But Tootsie disagreed, and seemed aggravated that I didn't immediately just abandon my desires to tell her she was right, as I so often had in the past. That ongoing conversation continued to cause friction between us.

During that same year, I had one of my best months ever at my company, and I decided to celebrate by going to the liquor store and buying a bunch of wine. The wine purchase totaled over $900, and when I told Tootsie, she proceeded to pitch a fit. Never mind the fact that I had paid for it all with money that I had earned. And my income was much higher than usual. Back when I had bought her three dresses that totaled $1500, she didn't even say thank you, let alone suggesting that I should save my money to help pay down my loans. Boy, how things had suddenly changed when I wanted to spend my money on myself!

And again, this was all my money. I had supported her while she was unemployed for 18 months after being fired from Mary Kay. And she had recently taken a position at the American Heart Association. But after a few months, she came home one day in tears and told me that she thought she was going to get fired. I asked why, and she said there was a personality clash between her and the VP. She gave me a story about how the VP was unreasonable and wouldn't listen to her ideas.

I realize now that the reason the American Heart Association was going to fire her was the same reason that Mary Kay ended up firing her: She was obsessed with being right. The fact that she'd rather be correct than happy made her very difficult to get along with. The American Heart Association had one president and five

VP's. She had started out reporting to the top VP at the organization, but they were already considering firing her after two months.

Luckily for Tootsie, they decided to give her a second chance, and so instead of firing her, they demoted her, so she would report to a lower-ranking VP on the East Coast. But it was clear that her personality was a detriment to her career and that she was challenging to get along with when she didn't get her way. She just continued to place more importance on being right than being happy. And what that translates to is that she had absolutely no reason to divorce me. We were completely happy together, but in 2019, for the first time, I had stopped letting her always be right. And that may have been enough for her to want to leave.

Although maybe it wasn't just that. In August of 2019, things started coming to a head, and many things were going on that I couldn't explain. For example, I noticed that she had begun getting many texts at all hours of the night. She brushed it off and said it was just her college friends being chatty, but I think she was probably lying to me about that.

She had also become increasingly stressed at work after being demoted, still living in constant fear of being fired for "Personality Clash." (Amazing how she had the same problem with two different VPs; I wonder who was the problem?) I counseled her and told her that we were making enough money from my business that she did not have to work at all, and it was not that big of a deal, so she didn't have to worry about being fired because I could easily support both of us – as I already had been. Looking back, I wonder if she was worried about not having her own income because she already knew that she was planning to leave me and not rely on my income.

Her absences from the house started to grow longer, and I sensed that she was growing distant. I was still very invested in saving the relationship, so I suggested that we go to couples therapy. Tootsie agreed, so in August of 2019, we contacted a therapist that I had used before and arranged an appointment.

At our first session, I explained why we were there and proceeded to lay out the difficulties we had been having, specifically Tootsie's behavior over the past year. She wouldn't admit to any of it, repeatedly denied everything I mentioned, from the late-night texting to the smaller amount of time she was spending at home. She said I was just imagining all of it and being ridiculous. She then accused me of everything she had been doing wrong: being controlling, losing interest in the relationship, etc.

The therapist said that it was good for us to hear how the other person felt and come back next week to start figuring out how to solve it. So, the next week we were back in the therapist's office, and once again, Tootsie was just there to lay all the blame at my feet and not take responsibility for anything. But having already gone over that the previous week, the therapist asked her to move past the blame game and start talking about how we could make things better.

Tootsie was utterly uninterested in doing that. I think the therapist agreed that she was unreasonable, but we'll never know for sure because we never went back for a third session. Tootsie just unilaterally decided that we were done with couples therapy, and wasn't willing to return. So that was the end of that attempt to solve things.

In August 2019, two of my staff members noticed something suspicious – although they wouldn't share this information with me until months later after the assault: Tootsie had suddenly purged me from her social media profile.

Previous to August, I was a pretty sizeable percentage of her social media feed. There were myriad photos of the two of us together, many of which had been taken on vacations that I had taken her on. I don't think we ever spent a single day in the Caymans where she wasn't posting to Instagram. And even when one of us had work, and we weren't in the same location, she'd often talk about me appreciatively on her feed. For good reason: I was very generous.

To give you an example, Queen was touring in Texas in 2018, and Tootsie wanted to go. I didn't see the point of seeing a band whose lead singer and most talented members were long since dead, but she was excited about it and had a group of girlfriends (The Big Five) she wanted to go with. So I pulled out all the stops. I not only bought tickets for her and her entire group of friends, but I also hired a private chauffeur bus to take them to the concert and even paid for all of them to have a nice dinner beforehand. They had a fantastic time, and Tootsie made a post on Facebook with a picture of her and all her girlfriends at the concert venue, thanking me for the wonderful treat.

Suddenly in August, everything Chuck-related disappeared from her social media. Big Facebook post thanking me for a fantastic concert party, gone. Hundreds of Instagram photos of us on vacation in the Caymans and elsewhere, gone. All pictures of me on any of her social media, all posts thanking me for the various gifts I had given her, all appreciation or even mention of our relationship, gone, gone, gone. It was like she had gone in and attempted to revise history by removing any trace of evidence that I had ever been in her life. And again, this was in August when we were still together – although my staff members noticed it, they wouldn't tell me about it until months later.

Meanwhile, although I had noticed a change in Tootsie's behavior, I had no idea that she was already planning to cut me out of her life. As far as I knew, this was just a bumpy patch that we would work through. To that end, I continued doing everything I could to keep her happy. We took another couple of trips to Scottsdale, Arizona, to see Wootsie for some more pleasure-filled weekends. In addition to the wild sex and threesomes, we had dinners at the most excellent restaurants and stayed at the nicest hotels. We alternated between having sex in the room and drinking top shelf at the pool bar – to the point where bar bills ended up running between $1,200-$1,800. Naturally, I paid for everything.

On the second Scottsdale trip in September, Tootsie's aunt and uncle came up to Scottsdale to join us for dinner. That dinner alone cost $700, and we had the two most excellent bottles of wine. And neither Wootsie, nor Tootsie, nor her family members ever offered to pay for anything. I always footed the bill.

But as much as everything continued to cost me, I figured it was all worth it if it would make Tootsie happy and save our relationship. Unfortunately, things kept trending in the wrong direction. The nauseating amount of text messages and pings late at night were starting to accelerate. She grew more distant – both figuratively, in terms of ignoring me when she was home, and literally, in that she was home a lot less often.

By October, it became apparent that Tootsie was just going through the motions, even to my lovesick self. She was now staying late at work every single day, and I had a hard time believing that they had suddenly entrusted her with that much extra work. Her cell phone was blowing up with constant text messages. And while she had once eagerly shared her texts and group texts with me, now she was hiding everything. We went to Napa in the first week of October, and she was completely disconnected. She seemed more interested in drinking wine than in actually spending any time with me, the person who had brought her there.

Once we got back from Napa, I had less than two weeks until I was due to go in for major back surgery. This was a complete L1-L4 overhaul of my back, steel rods and spacers, the whole nine yards. Tootsie had gotten involved with planning the surgery and then my care and rehabilitation, stepping up to be a fully supportive wife in a way I wasn't used to.

Not that the sex wasn't great; it was. But as far as being a best friend or being intimate in an emotional way instead of just physically, it never really happened. That essential deep personal connection just wasn't there. I was in love with her, but I couldn't confide in her. (I also couldn't trust her, but I learned that lesson far too late.)

So despite our incredible sexual chemistry, we were never incredibly close. But as 2019 wore on, she grew more and more distant over time. And to this day, I still don't know why. The most likely explanation I can think of is that she had an extramarital relationship. That wouldn't have surprised me. There was undoubtedly an uptick in weird communication and frequent text messages that were not there before. And I also knew from conversations reasonably early on in our relationship that she had had multiple extramarital affairs in her previous marriage – not to mention the "sex contests" with her one-night-stand friend in Denton, Texas.

Given all that, I would never be surprised that Tootsie might be having sex with other people. But what would surprise me if that were the case was the idea that she would feel compelled to lie about it. I don't understand why she would feel the need to hide anything from me. I had always encouraged her to explore sexually as long as I was involved. I had arranged threesomes for her with other women. From porn shops to Craigslist, I had made it crystal clear that Tootsie was welcome to have sex with other people. So I don't understand why she would feel the need to hide anything from me. As long as I could oversee it, I would have been happy to let her have sex with whoever she liked.

But while I may never know why she didn't have the spine to tell me what was going on, back in August, all I knew is that my spine was due for a massive surgery. Tootsie had promised to take care of me and handle everything while I was recovering, so I had stopped worrying about it and was trying to enjoy myself until operation day. To that end, we had invited some friends over on a Sunday night to watch the Cowboys game.

Yuri and Caesar were a couple that Tootsie and I had enjoyed dinner with a few times before, and they were always pleasant company. Tootsie made a fantastic meal, and we had two great bottles of wine between the four of us as we watched the game. After the game was over, we enjoyed more wine out in our beautiful side yard. Caesar and I talked about business while the girls cleaned the kitchen, and I mentioned my back surgery. He wished me well and said that he had gotten back surgery some years prior. He asked me what I was planning to do in terms of rehabilitation, and offered to recommend a physical therapist. I told him I had planned to go to the yoga studio and soak in a lot of heat, which he agreed was a good idea. Then Yuri and Tootsie returned from their walk, and Yuri said that she was tired, so she and Caesar decided to go home.

As we were cleaning up the dishes, I mentioned that Caesar had gotten back surgery and had helped me feel less worried about it.

I said I felt good about my plan of going to the yoga studio during my recovery period. Tootsie turned to look at me and told me that I should reconsider my plans. She said that she did not want me to do yoga or even go back to sit in the yoga studio's heat during my rehabilitation period. Rather, she felt I should be planning my recovery around the local fitness center that I used to go to. "Instead of yoga," she said, "you should be doing a treadmill or Stairmaster. That's going to be much better for your recovery."

I was unconvinced and told her so. First, I explained, I had been attending the yoga studio for the better part of the past decade (with Tootsie for the past five years), so all of my friends and people who cared about me were there. Meanwhile, I hadn't been to that health club in nearly eight years, in no small part precisely because I preferred the yoga studio.

And secondly, I knew it would probably be some weeks after the surgery before I was ready to jump on a treadmill or Stairmaster. As every yogi knows, the hot yoga room's heat is healing and probably the best thing for immediately after major lower back surgery. "Plus, I already talked with the owner," I said, "And I've gotten approval to just come into the room and sit down for as long as I need to, without straining myself by trying to push too early."

At this point, she glared at me and then suddenly stormed off because she was not getting her way. She gave me zero reason to return to the gym. There was no proof that a treadmill or Stairmaster would help me more than yoga – and every reason to believe that the opposite was true. I think that she simply wanted to oppose me. Although in retrospect, I wonder if she was having an affair with someone in our yoga studio and did not want me to return for that reason. That would be quite the bookend on our relationship if it were the case.

Regardless of the reason, she had stormed off after I announced that I had every intention of sticking with my plan to use the hot yoga studio for my post-surgery recovery. I waited about 5-7 minutes and let her cool down. I walked back into the kitchen, and she was standing over the big sink doing dishes. I calmly said to her, "Can we talk this out? I don't understand your reasoning." I was standing behind her, between the sink and the island in the middle of the kitchen. It was at that point that she turned around and, out of nowhere, physically assaulted me.

The assault was a violent rage. Tootsie started screaming at the top of her lungs, and at the same time, she took her fists and violently beat on my face and chest. Each time she raised her fists back up to strike me again, her nails scraped against the sides of my face. I don't remember what she was screaming. She was drunk and incoherent. I never defended myself; I just stayed still. I didn't have time to think; it all happened so fast.

Tootsie is only 5' and weighed 100 lbs., so two glasses of wine were usually plenty to put her under. That night she had already drunk at least 4-5 glasses. That fact was verified by the two friends who had just left 10-15 minutes before this whole explosion. So obviously, Tootsie was very drunk during this entire assault. I say that not to excuse it at all, but just to be honest about the whole situation.

After about 30 seconds of this drunken assault, she suddenly stops hitting me, stops screaming at me, runs up the stairs, and yells down that she is leaving. I was stunned and completely taken by surprise. I was in such a state of shock that I had to mentally replay the last minute of what had happened, to realize that I had been violently and physically assaulted.

I worked as a police officer paramedic for five years in a previous life. So I knew better than even to put my arms across my chest because this could have been taken as an offensive move. I am trained in self-defense, but instead of defending myself, I stood there and took it. I let her wail on me. I didn't follow her upstairs because, at this point, she was acting crazy. And I didn't see the point in trying to talk to a person whose blood alcohol was probably twice the legal limit.

I wasn't sure what to do. While she was upstairs, I thought for a few moments and then called the Carrollton PD. I told the police that I believed I had been assaulted, that we had been drinking, and that she was packing to leave. I was worried because I knew Tootsie was in no state to drive, and I told the police that. The dispatcher told me to stay put and that they were sending two units out immediately. I thanked them and hung up.

There was a period of probably a minute to two minutes where nothing was going on. Then Tootsie came back downstairs and said, "I am leaving." She had two bags in her hands and went down the stairs, ready to head out the door.

I said, "If you leave now, you are going to get arrested for DWI. I just called the police, and they are on their way." As soon as I said that, she dropped the two bags she had in her hands. I told her, "Stay here. I am going to wait in the garage for the officers. As soon as they get here, I will greet them, and then they will come and talk to you."

I walked past her and waited in the garage. When the police arrived, they came down the alleyway with their lights out. The lead officer got out of the car, walked up to me standing just inside the dark garage, and with his flashlight on me, he said, "Do you know, Mr. Bauer, that you have a black eye" I said no. He also said, "Did you know you had scratches on both sides of your face?" I said no. Then he asked me to tell him what happened. I told him everything just as I described it here, starting with the argument over the yoga studio, right up until the police arrived to meet me in the garage.

After hearing my entire story, the lead officer then entered the house and interviewed Tootsie. 7-8 minutes later, the officer came back into the garage and said to me, "Mr. Bauer, Mrs. Bauer has assaulted you, and we can go ahead and file charges and book her immediately for assault." That immediately told me that she told the police officer the truth. I was shocked that the master spin doctor didn't lie or try to spin what had happened for once. Maybe she was too drunk to bullshit the police.

The lead officer asked me what I would like to do. I said, "Can you give me 4-5 minutes? Because I want to think this through." I knew what we were talking about was an arrest record and a criminal complaint, and something that would affect her for the rest of her life. I wasn't just deciding what I wanted right now; I had to look at things and how it would impact her for the rest of her life (even though she never gave me the same courtesy). In the end, I decided that I was not going to press charges. My internal hope was that she would calm down, and after a couple of days, would come home so we could get this thing figured out.

The police officers noted that I refrained from filing charges, but still gave me 365 days to file charges against her if I changed my mind. Because of her lack of sobriety, the police decided to call a police Uber and set her up in a police-authorized hotel. She was still free and not under arrest, but could not leave the hotel until she had slept it off. They didn't tell me the hotel, nor did I care to ask. I was still in shock. I had never been assaulted before. I was confused. What was the real story? Why had she exploded at me out of nowhere? Was it really about my wanting to have rehabilitation at my yoga studio instead of the gym? Looking back, I think there must have been something else going on. In hindsight, I get the feeling she already had a foot out the door and had started planning to leave me back in August.

The police Uber arrived and took Tootsie away, and the officers said to me that everything had been recorded. They said that based on her comments, it was a pretty clear-cut case. They went over the police report with me and then left.

I walked back into the house, and I was still feeling shocked, completely off-center. I could not believe what had just happened. I was still in denial for a few moments. After revisiting how everything went, I then realized that I still feared for my safety. When Tootsie assaulted me, it was like I was dealing with a whole different person I didn't know. When I realized that, I became fearful that additional harm would come to me. I knew that she probably still had her garage door opener and that if she had taken it with her, she could use it to gain access to the house. I disconnected the electricity to the garage door and used a chair to bar the front door, just to be safe. I satisfied myself that there was no way that she (or anyone else) could gain access to the house.

The next morning, Tootsie showed up at the house. She texted me and asked me if she could gain access to the house. I said yes, but only as long as she has someone else with her and that she doesn't touch me. Tootsie said yes, her best friend Erin was already right there with her, and she just wanted to come in, get her personal belongings, and leave. I agreed, so the two of them came in and loaded up two cars with every last bit of Tootsie's clothing and personal items, removing them all from the house. Neither of them said a single word to me. I stood there in disbelief and watched as Tootsie loaded up five years of gifts that I bought for her. She wasn't just packing up her stuff. She was packing up half a decade of my life, our entire relationship, and driving it all away. It still almost didn't seem real to me, but at the same time, it was all too real and all too awful. You can't imagine the feeling.

After she left, I felt like I needed some support, so I called the National Domestic Violence Hotline. They were accommodating, recommended some places in Dallas for help, and told me to call them any time I needed them. Most of the people who operated the Hotline are former victims of domestic violence, so they understand what a traumatizing ordeal it is to go through. I appreciated their support at one of the lowest times in my life, which is why I decided that 50% of the proceeds of this book will go to support the National Domestic Violence Hotline and the excellent work that they do.

For photos of the police report and my injuries from the incident, you can visit:

https://100shadesofdeception.com/evidence/

CHAPTER 9:

THE DIVORCE

SIX DAYS WENT BY. AFTER I HAD RECOVERED ENOUGH to feel safe contacting Tootsie again, I reached out via phone calls and text messages to reconnect with her. I wanted to talk about what was going on and put together some plan to figure things out and get the relationship back on track. Even though she had assaulted me, I still loved her and wanted to save the relationship if there was any way we could do so. I suggested we try marriage counseling. But I got no response from her to that or any of the other messages. She ignored all my texts and wouldn't answer any of my phone calls. Finally, just two days before I was due to go in for that major back surgery, I got a text message from her. It was only a single line. It read:

"You are on your own for the surgery. I have filed for divorce."

This was devastating to me, on multiple levels. First, the plan up until that point had been that Tootsie would be my primary care-taker after the surgery. Before these unimaginable events happened, she had said Wootsie would come in and visit to hang out and help with the rehabilitation. Since Wootsie had always been closer to

Tootsie, I had no doubt that Wootsie would be seeing her instead of me after the split. And of course, Tootsie had just announced that she wouldn't be there for me either. After I got this text, I realized I was 48 hours away from having major back surgery, had been sued for divorce, and I had no one to help me.

My sister and her husband were scheduled to fly out to Dallas in two or three weeks and spend some time with me while Tootsie went to work. I called them and told them what happened, and they were shocked. They said that they would help me out any way they could and were willing to fly here immediately if I didn't have anyone local to take care of things. I didn't. So, I called American Airlines, and at the cost of $4,800, I arranged for them to fly in at the last minute and arrive the night of my surgery.

But as devastated as I was by suddenly being left with no caretakers after my surgery, I was at least as upset by Tootsie's complete abandonment of our relationship and her announcement that she was filing for divorce. After everything I had done for her, all the vacations I had taken her on, all the amazing experiences I had given her or paid for her to have, she just wanted to throw our whole relationship away like a sack of moldy tangerines. Even after she assaulted me, I was willing to forgive her and try to work things out between us. But she just wasn't interested and had no desire to talk to me.

Still, I wanted to talk to her because I wasn't willing to give up on her. So the very next day, I drove over to Tootsie's parents' house unannounced. I knew if I told them I was coming over to talk, they would probably just tell me not to come at all, and I had to take one last shot at staying in this marriage. I never wanted to get divorced, so I was going to do everything in my power to prevent it from happening.

I showed up at her parents' house and knocked on the door. Her father answered the door and invited me in. He said that they had convened a family council, and the family had determined that Tootsie should divorce me and leave me. I was incensed. I always knew that Tootsie's family influenced her, but I never imagined that the family would somehow meet and decide who she should be married to. Indeed, it's not like Tootsie consulted them before deciding to be with me instead of her previous husband. But I had been nothing but generous with them, and to be repaid for that with a "family council" telling Tootsie to divorce me was hurtful. I asked her father to serve as a go-between and set up a way for me to talk to Tootsie to make things right. He refused to lift a finger to help me, just shook his head and said there was nothing he could do. This was the last straw.

I said, "I find it ironic that I am sitting here in front of a man that is involved with boy scouts, and constantly around young children and men, and has been accused by not one, but two of your wife's sisters of raping them, one 20 years ago and one just two years ago when I met you. And yet I supported you through all of that, even though everyone was saying terrible things about you. And here I am being expelled from this family thanks to your 'family council' when I haven't done anything except support and love your daughter and given her everything she wants. I have laid $50,000 of jewelry on her(total), allowed her to be unemployed for 18 months, and provided her a nearly debt-free existence. I let her have her sexual shenanigans with girlfriends and provided her with emotional support. I have taken her to travel around the world, with nothing but the best dinners, and stays at the most excellent hotels. I have been the friend, boyfriend, and husband that she always wanted, by her own words. She didn't even have the guts to tell me that she fell out of love with me and tried to leave me. And you can't even be bothered to let me have one conversation with her to try to save our marriage? Where do you draw the line?"

I was so frustrated that I just turned around, walked off, and left him standing there. But it's not like he was going to say anything else; he had already made it very clear that he was going to be completely useless. One of the most terrible drives of my life was that drive home after talking to her father. How dare he. How dare they. A family of people who felt like they could do no wrong, making judgment calls like that. I knew then that I had no shot whatsoever at staying in the marriage.

I was furious at her family at the time, and although I still am, I have since realized that it may not have been entirely their fault. After everything I had done for Tootsie and everything I had done for them, I was angry that they could just discard all that over nothing. But what I didn't think of at the time was that I hadn't been in constant contact with her family, and the Spin Doctor had. The odds that Tootsie had told them the truth of everything that had happened were utterly nil. I do not doubt that they were fed stories that probably made me look like a comic book villain, and if that was the case, then it's perhaps not too surprising that they told her to divorce me.

I woke up early the next morning at 6 am and drove myself to the hospital for my surgery. They put me under for the operation, and when I came to, it was 3 am the next day. My sister and her husband were there, as were my two best friends Joe and Sheri. They had all arrived while I was in surgery and were there to make sure I didn't have to go through all of this alone. Having family and true friends to support me in my hour of need was wonderful, and I especially appreciated it after having Tootsie abandon me.

I still couldn't believe that Tootsie refused to so much as talk to me. Ironically, although she was refusing to talk to me, she was perfectly happy to talk to my personal assistant. Within a few days of my going in for surgery, my personal assistant received a phone call from Tootsie. Since I was in the hospital, Tootsie wanted my personal assistant to give her access to the house, just so she could get a few of her things. My personal assistant, ever an excellent judge of character, declined.

Tootsie called back later that same afternoon, and once again requested to have access to my house in order to retrieve her things. Thank goodness that my personal assistant was suspicious, and flat-out refused her again. But Tootsie would not be deterred. Over the next few days, she launched a campaign of phone calls designed to manipulate my personal assistant into granting her access to the house.

I have no doubt that if Tootsie had been granted access to the house, she'd have taken everything that wasn't nailed down. I know she wanted to clean out my kitchen, where every fork, spoon, mixing bowl, and top of the line piece of chef equipment was all expensive stuff paid for by me because she had wanted it. I was pretty sure she still wanted it and was trying to manipulate my personal assistant into letting her pilfer it all, but thankfully my assistant was made of sterner stuff.

And good thing that was the case, because after a few days of Tootsie's unsuccessful attempts to call up my personal assistant to gain access, Tootsie deployed her secret weapon: Her mother. Yes, Tootsie's mother jumped in on the action and joined Tootsie in sending calls and messages to my personal assistant, once again trying to manipulate her into granting them access to the house.

My personal assistant was appalled by the whole situation and shocked that anyone would be so brazen about it. Here I was in the hospital for an 11-hour surgery, basically unconscious for two days, completely laid up and unable to move – after which I still had a few days poking around the hospital with a walker and gown – and meanwhile Tootsie and her mother were just calling up and bombarding my personal assistant with messages to try to get into my house before I recovered enough to definitively tell them no.

My life was in complete upheaval due to Tootsie's actions. If my family hadn't flown in to stay there with me – on a $4800 last-minute flight – I don't know what would have happened. Frankly, I believe that if nobody had been there to protect it, that Tootsie would have considered just raiding the house in an attempt to get my things. I was fortunate to have people I can rely on – my family, who were willing to drop everything and fly out to take care of me when I needed it, and my personal assistant, who knew better than to accept a sob story and let the woman who had betrayed me into my house.

I was in the hospital for six days before I was finally released. Once they let me out, I came home, and my sister and her husband stayed with me for two weeks to take care of me through the recovery. The first Friday night after the surgery, I had just finished having a home-cooked dinner that my sister was kind enough to make for me when I remembered that Tootsie had told me that Wootsie would be in town, and they were planning a weekend at the Ritz. Initially, they were also supposed to help with post-surgery recovery, but obviously, that wasn't happening. Yet I couldn't help but wonder whether Tootsie's split with me meant that Wootsie's trip had been canceled, or if Wootsie was still going to visit and have a party but just stay with Tootsie and pretend I didn't exist.

That Friday at 8:30 pm, I called the Ritz in downtown Dallas and asked if Tootsie and Wootsie were registered there. They said yes. So, while I was laid up and could barely move, my former wife was with our lover (who was also a former client of mine), celebrating at the Ritz. It hurt even worse than my back.

Still, knowing that Wootsie was there with Tootsie meant that I had an opportunity. I knew Tootsie had already made it clear that she didn't want to talk to me again of her own free will. I had already given up convincing Tootsie's family to help push Tootsie into talking with me. Wootsie represented my last hope of convincing Tootsie to at least have a conversation with me so we could talk things out and try to salvage our relationship. And I figured if anyone close to Tootsie had reason to listen to me and urge her to at least talk to me, it was Wootsie. After all, I had been everything to Wootsie: Instructor, lover, and sugar daddy. She had enjoyed all sorts of memorable vacations, experiences, and sex-filled weekends with Tootsie and me, all on my dime. Surely she would see reason and tell Tootsie it was at least worth hearing me out.

So I texted Wootsie and asked her to intervene to get Tootsie back to talking with me again. She replied, "Sorry, Tootsie asked me not to get in the middle of things." I responded that it was far too late for that because she had already been in the middle of things for some time. To that, she did not respond. I told her that I knew where they were, living it up at the Ritz while I was across town recovering from back surgery. She blocked my number and refused to talk to me.

The next day I was able to get a receipt emailed to me and found out that the room was paid for and purchased by Wootsie. Tootsie once again was using other people's money instead of her own. How ironic that her family was in mourning over her having to get a divorce while she was shacked up in the Ritz with her girlfriend, Wootsie. This was the thanks that I got.

Not only had I been through major surgery, I still had to run my company because I am the company. There's no Chuck Bauer's Business Development Training without Chuck Bauer. So, while I might have liked to take another few weeks to recuperate, I went back to work. Now during this same period, I had the added pleasure of working on the divorce. Unlike Tootsie, I did not have any family or friends in town to help me out. I was lucky enough to have my sister and her husband and Joe and Sheri help me after the surgery, but I was on my own when it came to the divorce.

I had gotten served electronically with the divorce papers two days before the surgery, but there was so much going on that I hadn't had time to deal with it yet. So I knew I needed to hire some legal representation.

I got referred to a law firm in Plano that was an all-woman team of lawyers, and when I interviewed them, they said they would be as tough as nails, and I didn't have anything to worry about. They also said that they knew Tootsie's attorney from working with her in the past. This would be a plus because they knew how this attorney worked and didn't work. After speaking to the attorneys, I found it very odd that they counseled me right away not to go ahead and have Tootsie arrested for the assault. I had a full year to file the charges, but they said I shouldn't do that. I later found out that this was ultimately the wrong advice.

After hiring my crack attorney team, I started to feel uneasy about the divorce's direction, because it seemed like it was all heavily weighted in Tootsie's favor. Because there was no prenuptial agreement, under Texas law (where we live), she stood to gain half of the community property -- even though she never contributed to it with any money of her own. It became clear that Tootsie just wanted more money from me. And I was starting to feel that the law firm that I had hired to represent my interests did not have my best interest at heart. The fact that they knew Tootsie's attorney was supposed to let them fight more effectively for me to keep my money, but so far, I wasn't impressed.

I felt as though things were just not going to go my way. I was at a loss because I had placed her first for five years and provided everything for her, and she completely took advantage of that. Every time I would try to discuss strategies with my lawyers, they seemed like they were against everything I suggested and not interested in fighting for me. I felt like I had no leverage to protect my interests or encourage them to do so. I raised the possibility of filing assault charges against Tootsie to use as a bargaining chip, but they shot it down.

It wasn't a fun period for me. A lot of it was personal despair. I began questioning everything that I had done for her. What had happened to my moral compass, that I had been willing to have all these wild shenanigans and go off doing things I would never have imagined doing, all to please her? There were many sleepless nights and days spent working non-stop and focusing on clients, which I hoped might help me take my mind off Tootsie and the divorce.

It didn't work. Mainly because every day seemed to bring a new Tootsie-related headache. We had scheduled a new year's trip to the

Caymans, and of course, she refused to pay for any of that, so it fell to me. We also had a trip booked to San Diego with her parents, where I had pre-paid for everything, and all of that had to be unwound as well. Trying to recover my money was turning out to be a nightmare.

She also had over $50,000 worth of jewelry I had purchased, and I asked for the jewelry to be returned but was told no. The most expensive piece was the $27,000 custom ring that I had purchased, mostly from Wootsie's jeweler. I specifically asked for this piece to be returned, as it represented the bulk of my jewelry investment, but Tootsie informed me (via her attorney) that I could not have it.

And as if all that wasn't enough, with all the effort I had to put into trying to reclaim the money I had already spent on Tootsie, it turned out that she was still trying to take more, even after leaving me! Somehow, Tootsie had illegally gained access to my business account. I found this out literally when I was in the middle of running a coaching session. My CPA firm had caught Tootsie trying to transfer money out of my business account, and thankfully they recognized that as a red flag. My firm notified me as soon as they realized what was happening, so I had to leave my meeting immediately and go down to the branch in person to sort things out. As a precautionary measure, we decided to have Chase shut down all five of my accounts. Thank goodness we did, because Tootsie could have done some severe damage, and I was lucky that my firm caught her before she got away with more of my money. But the downside of shutting down all my accounts was that it pretty much put me entirely out of financial operations for about 48 hours, which is very inconvenient when you are trying to run your own business. It was a giant mess to recreate everything, but a few days later, I was up and running again, and we soldiered on.

A couple of weeks before all of this happened – and I say a couple of weeks because that's how time works, but keep in mind that from my perspective, it was also basically an entire lifetime ago – Tootsie and I had met up with Wootsie for a secret rendezvous or two in Scottsdale. At my expense, naturally. I was spending somewhere between $1,300 and $1,800 per day just on food and drink. We were living it up with our wild sex parties and top-shelf lifestyle as usual, and I thought we'd continue doing this forever. Simultaneously, Tootsie had already decided that she would leave me in a matter of weeks – even though she had given me no indication that anything was wrong.

I figured that if Tootsie (and possibly Wootsie, who I strongly suspect she told) had already been planning on leaving me at that point, that I shouldn't be on the hook for all those expensive weekends. I asked if Tootsie and Wootsie would pay back 1/3 of those bills, but the answer was no. I footed the bill for her sex weekends and her family's meals, even though she knew that within less than three weeks, she would be walking out on me. And I have to presume that she had already planned to leave me because I cannot believe that the big event that would push her to want to leave me would be me wanting to let the heat of my long-time yoga studio heal me and contribute to my rehabilitation.

After four months, we went to mediation. Having gotten my back and accounts all returned to full working order, I was quite busy running my business and dealing with clients. I had to pay extra to my CPA firm to get all of my financials done for the mediation. The morning of the mediation, 10 minutes before I left, I got a last-minute phone call from my attorney informing me that the mediator was sick and would not perform the mediation.

Instead, she suggested that the attorneys perform the mediation, so Tootsie's attorney and my attorneys would hash things out at my attorney's office – where I should show up post-haste. So, I arrived at the office and was sequestered in a conference room. It turned out that Tootsie and her attorney were in the other conference room 150 ft away, which I found out while I was taking a break, walked down a hallway, and saw her. She had her back to me and never even saw me there. I couldn't help but think how ironic it all was. This is what it all came down to. Millions of flight miles, tens of thousands of dollars, and thousands of experiences, and it all came down to this.

Before we head into the mediation, I felt like I was running into a brick wall being told no by my attorneys. I found out is that this was not a mediation (since the mediator was unavailable) but a negotiation. Once again, I asked if I could have the arrest warrant executed on her, and my attorneys said, "No, it would make you look vindictive." I just figured that if this was a negotiation, I should have some leverage to recover some financial loss. But I was told in no uncertain terms to forget about pressing charges and executing the arrest warrant. I didn't want to look vindictive and needed to trust my attorneys to negotiate to my best advantage.

Once we begin the negotiation, I lost what little faith I had remaining in my attorneys. They were negotiating everything Tootsie wanted, but it seemed like whenever I raised things that I wanted, we couldn't negotiate. The settlement ended up where she wanted our $12K inventory of wine and the wine refrigerator custom-built into our house, plus she kept all the jewelry and gifts. Unwillingly, I signed the divorce papers. They told me it was the best that I was going to get. Tootsie signed as well, and then it was done.

The only thing that went my way in that entire negotiation was that Tootsie had to pay me $6,700 to reimburse travel expenses because I put enough pressure on the attorney about the trips and rooms that I had to cancel in the Grand Caymans and San Diego. I wondered how these "Tough as nails" attorneys could be so ineffective at negotiating what I wanted. Come to find out, my attorneys and Tootsie's were in bed together. They were walking around laughing and giggling with their shoes off. The whole thing was a joke, but at least it was finally over.

Looking back, it's clear that not having the right legal staff at the beginning likely fueled a lot of the issues I had with Tootsie. I'm currently filing a grievance with the state of Texas against my attorneys because they were so utterly useless. Or I guess more accurately, they completely sucked and were useless for me, but were certainly useful for Tootsie, since they seemed to be in bed with her attorneys, and succeeded in making sure I got the fuzzy end of the lollipop in our divorce settlement.

It just goes to show, when the chips are down, everything depends on having quality people on your side. Obviously, those attorneys were terrible. But I was carried throughout this ordeal by my family, and my loyal personal assistant. When my personal assistant told me about all the attempted manipulations, I could only shake my head. My personal assistant has never been into any kind of drama and has been my trusted and loyal assistant for a decade.

And my personal assistant is actually my newest staff member. I've had almost no turnover since I started slowly hiring staff in 2003, then another team member in 2006, and my current personal assistant back in 2010. I treat my staff very well. In fact, they're all vested with me in my insurance, so if I kick the bucket, they're taken care of. They know I'm looking out for them, and they look out for me. That's how I've gone for nearly two decades with no turnover. That's the kind of loyalty I built within my company, the kind of loyalty that it's clear Tootsie doesn't understand.

In an ideal relationship, your partner should be the person you trust most in the world. You should be able to know unquestionably that your partner will always have your back. But while obviously my personal assistant was loyal to me, it was very clear that Tootsie never had my best interests in mind. The only person she ever had in mind was herself. Or when she did have other people in mind, it was only to satisfy her own sexual urges. Which certainly explains her sex-filled getaway the week of my surgery.

I just find it so interesting that after the surgery, when I was laid up at home where I could barely move, under heavy medication, with friends and family flying in from all over the country to help out... here was the prom queen (or shall we say PORN QUEEN?) eagerly meeting Wootsie, who flies in from Phoenix, so they could get together for their little Ritz Romp Sex Weekend. And shockingly, that was when the phone calls to my personal assistant (all being made in an effort to gain access to the house) mysteriously ceased. Well played, Tootsie, well played.

The Yoga Community (All In Denial)

Tootsie and I were both very involved in the yoga community in Dallas. We had, of course, met through yoga and continued doing yoga together throughout our relationship. After Tootsie assaulted me and then stonewalled me, news that we were getting a divorce began to spread among the yoga community. Unfortunately, the primary way that it spread must have been Tootsie telling people, because more often than not, when I saw a friend in the yoga world who I hadn't spoken to since before the incident, they already knew about the divorce before I could tell them.

The downside of this was that everyone had heard the story from the Spin Doctor herself, rather than hearing what happened from me. And even when I tried to explain my side of the story, our mutual friends (with a few notable exceptions) completely dismissed the truth of what had happened. Despite the years I had known these people, almost all of them were unwilling to give me the benefit of the doubt and hear me out. They just heard Tootsie spin her version of the story and immediately decided I must have been entirely at fault.

No one looked at the fact that Tootsie had physically assaulted me, creating contusions on my shoulder and chest, scratches up and down my face, and an excellent black eye. I tried to point this out to people, but they had no interest in listening. They couldn't believe that domestic violence could ever come from a small 5' woman attacking me, a 6' man. The existence of a full-blown police report supporting my description of events (and presumably contradicting Tootsie's) did nothing to change their minds about the facts of the case. All of my pleas for understanding fell on deaf ears. I got no sympathy.

It seemed that I was just too late. The Spin Doctor had already worked her magic here, turning many of my long-time yoga friends against me, and there was nothing I could do about it. I felt like it was so fake for people just to take her side, but the damage had been done. Only four or five people even asked how I was doing or checked on me to make sure I was okay. Nobody else seemed to care about me at all anymore.

Eventually, I had to leave the studio where I had done yoga for years, simply because I no longer felt comfortable practicing around so many people who had turned against me. It seemed like a cruel irony that I suffered the assault and ended up shunned by my community, while Tootsie was the one guilty of the domestic violence. Yet, somehow she was welcomed with open arms like a prom (porn?) queen who had been the victim, even though the truth was precisely the opposite. Even as I write this, almost a year later, many of my former yoga friends are still acting as though she did nothing wrong, and I was the one at fault.

All I can say is, Tootsie is an incredibly skilled Spin Doctor. It honestly leaves me in awe. How do you spin the fact that you were within inches of being arrested and could have been imprisoned for up to a full year for an apparent case of domestic assault – and then manage to make yourself the victim and make me the villain? That is some high-grade severe spin. If I had been the one that attacked her, it would have been a completely different story. But that is not what happened. For really no reason at all, she struck me, and then managed to convince our yoga friends that I was at fault. I would be impressed if it hadn't left me so depressed.

And her negative effect on my network of connections didn't stop with the yoga community. It had a severe impact on my business and networking as well. Through my coaching business, I've managed to build up a fantastic clientele of over 1,500 people. That network of 1,500 people represents the years of hard work I've put into my business, into marketing myself and making connections.

Through my seminars, social media, and occasional vacations where she met clients in person, Tootsie was probably personally known to about half of my clientele. As far as they were concerned,

Chuck and Tootsie were a package deal. Well, when Tootsie exploded and irrationally decided not to stay married to me anymore, I mostly kept quiet about it. I figured I didn't need to broadcast my personal life's tragedies to all of my business clients.

What I hadn't counted on was that by not saying anything to get out in front of it, I was leaving everyone to ask me about it. I had hundreds of people asking me, "Where's Tootsie?" Wondering why she disappeared, disappointed not to see her by my side as they had become accustomed to.

When it came to my inner circle -- the long-running coaching clients I considered good friends, who knew Tootsie and me reasonably well -- I suffered abandonment across the board. Everyone wants to do business with a winner. But people were a lot less excited about being coached on how to run a successful business by a guy who apparently couldn't run a successful marriage. They didn't care that it wasn't my fault and that I'd done everything possible to make her happy. They just knew that they were friends with Chuck and Tootsie, and now Chuck and Tootsie were no longer an item.

People were in shock and dismay, and as much as that was inconvenient for my social life, it was even more problematic for my business life. For a while, it seemed like nobody wanted to ask about my business services. All they wanted to ask about was Tootsie. And that negatively affected my business, in a dramatic way. For all the contingency plans a small business has in place, from having built-in redundancies to holding a cash reserve, there's no contingency plan for a family crisis. There's no book I'm aware of to explain how a small business is supposed to deal with a severe relationship crisis like this and how it affects you. This caused a tremendous amount

of upheaval for me, and it took me nearly a year to try to
it and get my business back on track.

To this day, I still get comments asking about Tootsie. I've pretty
much disappeared from social media, in large part specifically to
avoid that, but the words keep coming. When Tootsie left me, it
caused a severe amount of damage to my life.

For photos of my injuries from the incident and other damage
that Tootsie caused me, you can visit:

https://100shadesofdeception.com/evidence/

For more evidence, just keep reading.

CHAPTER 10:
THE AFTERMATH.

WHILE I WAS DISAPPOINTED AT BEING LARGELY ABAN-
doned by the Dallas yoga community, I did have people who cared
about what I went through. After the divorce, several friends, family,
and clients of mine sympathized not only with the original ordeal I
went through with Tootsie, but the subsequent badmouthing of me
that Tootsie was doing in the community.

Some of them came to me and asked if there was any way
that they could help in terms of getting the truth out about what
happened. I told them that I was totally on board with that, and it
would come as a great comfort to me because so far, the spin queen
was able to spin lies upon lies upon lies, and it worked so well that I
no longer felt welcome in my yoga studio. Nobody knew about the
assault, the police report, or any of the other facts of the case that
probably didn't match up with whatever story Tootsie was telling.

That group of people got a copy of the certified public record
police report, along with pictures of my injuries and other corrob-
orating evidence, and made up little releases that they sent out to

various people and organizations in our spheres to try to set the record straight. These information packets created waves in Tootsie's life because my side of the story was now being told, and she didn't like the truth running up against her spin.

After she got blindsided by the police reports, her attorney tried to have papers served on me for a temporary restraining order. So thanks to that, I am not supposed to have communication with her family members anymore. And just to make it a full sweep, I also had to agree not to contact Wootsie after the mediation negotiations. Wootsie owed me money from the sexcapade trips and ended up being represented by Tootsie's attorney. When was the last time you heard of a divorce where the same attorney represented two women against one man?

It was all so unimaginable, and the whole saga was unbelievable. And indeed, thanks to Tootsie's spin-doctoring, very few people believed it. But I was fortunate that I had friends who assembled some of the evidence backing up the facts and sent it out. And I now want to share some of that evidence with you.

After my surgery, I ended up sending out the following release because I wanted to keep the record straight:

Tootsie and I separated after an incident here at our home in late October. I would not agree with her plans for post-surgery care. She wanted me to go back to my old health club. I wanted to get back to the hot room and heal slowly. The studio owner had already agreed to my plans, and I wanted the healing effects of being surrounded by a hot room as well as my friends and yoga acquaintances during my recovery.

In the flash of a moment, the discussion turned into a sudden, drunken, VIOLENT RAGE! She screamed at the top of her lungs and assaulted me, resulting in a black eye, scratches on my face, welts on my chest, and a significant contusion on my left shoulder. (I have pictures.) I NEVER touched her or placed a hand on her. It happened very fast. From her screaming numerous times and striking me with both fists, I'm sure that her actions perfectly fit the "violent rage" description.

After assaulting me, she ran upstairs and packed two bags. As she was heading out to drive away, I notified her that she was under the influence of alcohol (she had consumed over a bottle of wine, as verified by friends who were here and had just left), that she shouldn't be driving, and that I had called the Carrolton PD. I told her to stay in the house while I went outside to wait for the dispatched officers.

Two officers with the Carrollton PD arrived. After interviewing both of us, they determined that (1) they could place her under immediate arrest for assault and book her, or (2) they could file a full report, which would be in the Carrollton Police files. I chose that they should file a full report and not make the arrest. Additionally, they gave her a verbal warning and advised her to leave the premises via Uber, as she was getting ready to drive under the influence. I have the full report if you would like to see it.

THE DAY BEFORE my major eight-hour back surgery, she filed for divorce and left me with absolutely no one at the hospital to be with me. At the cost of $4800, I had to fly in family members the next evening to be here for two weeks to assist in my post-care. The back surgery lasted eight hours.

A week later, while I was entirely laid up recovering from my surgery, I was informed that Tootsie and her girlfriend/partner were planning a THREE-DAY RITZ ROMP weekend at the Downtown Dallas Ritz Hotel. Her partner, who resides in Phoenix, flew in on this particular evening, and Tootsie picked her up from DFW before proceeding to the Ritz.

After being advised of their plans, I texted her partner while they were driving to the Ritz. I told the partner that I knew of their three-day plans at the Ritz and that she was getting in the middle of our marriage. Her partner blocked my number and refused to talk to me.

Tootsie took a trip to NYC in August with her niece. One of my staff members was excited to see her Instagram pictures upon Tootsie's return. When the staff member went to see her trip pictures, she noticed that all of our joint images (CB & Tootsie) had been removed, and at the same time, she said that Tootsie had replaced her main IG picture with what looked like a high school yearbook picture.

The staff member never said anything until Tootsie left. In a written statement to my legal team, the staff member stated that it now looks like a deliberate attempt to sabotage the marriage as she was looking for something else. She was setting up her departure from the relationship.

Additionally, she secretly accessed my computer and removed all of my files on her. I did not discover this until AFTER she had left. A few weeks after that, I get a frantic phone call from my CPA, indicating that Tootsie was caught with FULL ACCESS (we have a picture of the screen visually showing that she had gained access to my business checking account.) We had evidence that she accessed my credit card accounts. My CPA directed me to immediately go to Chase and have her blocked while changing my accounts to new account numbers.

For over two years, she wanted to do the house remodel. I finally gave in and proceeded with her wishes. Did she offer financial support to the project? (Again, at this point, any money she had made was stashed in her retirement accounts.) Of course, NOT!

Because of her PR background, she controls very different narratives with different people. Her truth can be in three forms, depending on who you are or what group you are attached to. This was displayed when her family had a brewing crisis, and Tootsie monitored all family communication through different email accounts and unique cell phone numbers.

WORSE, SHE HAD FILED TO GET HALF OF THE COMMUNITY PROPERTY when she paid for absolutely NOTHING for five years. I supported her fully during that time. She contributed absolutely no financial support to the relationship or family finances. She was dismissed from her job at Mary Kay (employer claimed she was challenging to work with). She was out of work for over a year while I took care of her needs. I am already $25,000 into my legal team. What a FOOL I was.

The last few months after the home remodel, she spent excessive time with her work, accepting phone calls, emails, and text messages AT ALL HOURS. She spent a HUGE amount of time taking care of the legal situation with her father and family. Her feelings at this point were also being diverted to her Scottsdale partner. I was the odd person out. And she refused counseling or any effort to try to remedy the situation. Of course she did. She had neither a financial nor emotional commitment — no skin in the game.

I guess at this point if you have any other questions, you can let me know. I am saddened and embarrassed about what has happened. There are different yoga friends at my studio who know the story along with a small group of my personal friends and clients. It has been a significant struggle and frankly a SHOCK that this took place. I entirely took care of her emotionally and financially for five years. She is in complete denial about anything (alcohol, assault, commitment) and accepts no responsibility.

I ask for your patience and understanding if I seem quiet or distracted. I am doing the very best that I can. Even better, her rage and the violent assault were enough to convince me to STOP DRINKING. The stress of the situation has caused me to lose twenty pounds. Since that fateful evening in October, I am happy to say that I have not had a drop of alcohol. So, I guess there is always a silver lining in the clouds.

That release was sent out to several people. But I still felt like most people hadn't gotten my side of the story and had only heard Tootsie's version of events. That's one of the big reasons I wanted to write this book.

Unfortunately, it appeared that I was alone on that. Probably 99% of the people who I spoke to about my idea for this book had said no, absolutely not, do not write this book. And I found that a little odd, considering this was my story about what I had gone through. People love stories about triumph over adversity, about people who go through a rough patch in their lives and get through it and come out stronger and put their lives back together. People love stories about victims of domestic violence who speak their truth and reclaim things on their own terms. And yet almost every single person I talked to told me not to write this book.

If I'm being honest, I think people were probably blowing off the domestic violence just because I'm a guy, and because I stood a foot taller than she did. People are very set on the idea that domestic violence victims are always women and not men. But that's not true. I was absolutely the victim in this event. When it happened, I never raised a fist to her, never even protected myself when she started hitting me. I thought if I tried to do anything, it could be thought of as an offensive act. So I just stood there while she hit me in a drunken rage.

The whole thing was actually captured on my home security camera, but that was erased after 30 days. Which is a shame, as it would have shown everyone how violent the attack was. But meanwhile, most people seemed to have a really hard time believing that I could have been the victim of domestic violence.

The exception was the wonderful staff at the Domestic Violence Hotline. When I called them – anonymously, of course – they were just really fabulous people who were willing to talk to me and help me get through a tough situation. Nobody there questioned the idea that the man could be the victim in a domestic violence situation. They know it happens. It's a really active group with a great purpose, and I hope to become a spokesperson someday.

But when it came to everyone else, they just couldn't accept that the guy could be the victim in my situation. It's really weird how everyone always just takes the side of the female, especially in this case. And I'm sure that's exactly what will continue to happen with her. I have no doubt her little friends and family will all gather around her as usual and enable her, automatically presuming that she's in the right and I'm in the wrong. I saw it happen many times before, even when she had her friend Footsie (who she was still sleeping with) come to the big Shrimp Boil every year with his wife and kids. Everyone still looked at her as perfect and took her side, just as they continue to do now that she has split up with me.

If anyone ever had a reason to stay in a marriage and work out minor communication issues, it was her. I gave her everything she could possibly ask for, but she simply had no interest in making it work. She just didn't do it. She basically drank a bottle of wine by herself, a clear sign of alcoholism, but she refuses to take responsibility. And I'm sick of everyone believing her version of events, which is why I needed to get my story out there, to represent myself in terms of what happened.

So when everyone I talked to about my idea for this book told me, "Chuck, don't write that book," I didn't care. People asked me, "Why are you doing this? What do you hope to gain? Don't you think this will look bad?" I don't care. I just care that my message gets out and that I can see myself represented in my story of what happened. I'm sick of the only story out there being her version of events, or the version of events people make up in their head because I'm the guy and I'm bigger so they automatically leap to conclusions. I needed to get my side of the story out there. So, I don't care if people like me or hate me; this is part of my healing process, to be able to tell the authentic story of what happened.

And it is also a big reason that Tootsie did NOT want me to write this book. She had been giving everyone her version of events, and really did not want my story to come out.

And that's for good reason – it turns out, reading my book changed people's minds who had initially thought I was in the wrong. I know this because I shared an early draft with a friend of mine, and she went from thinking perhaps I had treated Tootsie too unkindly, to thinking that Tootsie was the one acting maliciously. I'll let her explain in her own words:

———

"The first time that I met Chuck, he was already married to Tootsie. He clearly held Tootsie in high esteem, always holding doors open for her, and generally attending to her every need. Chuck was always openly affectionate with Tootsie, while she tended to be more reserved. Still, they seemed to be a very established couple, which is why it came as a surprise to me when I heard that they were getting divorced.

The next time I saw Chuck, I offered him condolences on his marriage ending. We had a conversation about Tootsie and everything that had led up to his divorce. As we continued talking, Chuck told me that he was going to write a tell-all book about his marriage and divorce. My first reaction was that it was a bad idea and that writing a book about it seemed like a mean thing to do. I told him that while it sounded like Tootsie had been malicious, she was obviously suffering or sick herself. If Chuck really loved Tootsie, I felt he should turn the other cheek and help her in her moment of need, instead of attacking her. Although Tootsie was suing him for divorce at the time, I suggested that he find it in his heart to be merciful and forgive her.

He told me that I didn't really understand the whole story and that because of social paradigms and the fact that Tootsie was lying her ass off, all their mutual friends still viewed Tootsie as the perfect cheerleader that could do no wrong and took her side. He said that I was asking him to forgive her without knowing the full story of how she had betrayed him in an evil manner. This, he said, was precisely why he *needed to tell the full story of what had happened. Because even I, as his friend, was approaching the situation by giving Tootsie the benefit of the doubt – which he clearly felt she did not deserve.*

I was not very close with Chuck or Tootsie, and therefore I felt I could be fair and impartial when it came to evaluating the story of what happened in their divorce. So, I asked Chuck to tell me the full story of what happened, so I could really understand. It became obvious to me that Tootsie had used Chuck, but Chuck had to take responsibility for allowing it to happen. He agreed to let his wife sleep around. He agreed to have an affair with her while she was still married to another man. He agreed to lavish her with gifts and trips. He kept telling me that he thought if he provided for her with everything she asked for, she would stay. But shouldn't he take responsibility for ignoring all the signs that pointed to Tootsie's fickle and depraved character? How could he be surprised that this woman had no loyalty to him, given that their relationship started in an affair? He was the one who chose to be with a woman like that, so I found it difficult to accept that he was the victim in all of this.

But that was before I had gotten the full story. As I mentioned, Chuck had decided to turn his story into an actual book, because he said it was the only way to get his story right. Once he had finished writing up a full draft of the book, he sent me a preliminary manuscript. I sat down and read the whole story cover to cover. It was only then that I realized how Tootsie had been intentionally malicious, and how Chuck was slowly deceived and tricked by this talented manipulator. When Chuck had initially told me about his divorce, I was unconvinced that he was really the victim. But after reading the whole story, I realized this woman is dangerous, and hopefully the book plays a role in stopping her behavior and waking her up to the consequences of using people and then discarding them.

More importantly, I hope this book helps to protect others from falling victim to a similar situation. It is truly a story of modern-day prostitution and the consequences that entails. At this point, I am no longer convinced that Tootsie ever really loved Chuck in the first place. It is unclear to me whether she is even capable of loving another person, at this point in her life. It might be the case that she just wants to use people for sex, and that love is a convenient excuse.

As you can see, even though I had told my friend all about my history with Tootsie, it was only after reading a draft of this book that she understood how I was the one who had been wronged, not Tootsie. When I saw how powerful my story could be to persuade people that Tootsie was the villain in this story, I knew I had to get it out and share it with more people.

That's also why Tootsie was so worried about me releasing this book. She had everyone believing her version of events, and knew that if everyone read this book, they'd stop believing her and start believing me. She did everything she could think of to try to prevent me from publishing this book.

In fact, she hired a lawyer to try to shut me up and stop me from publishing this book. You can see the letter I was sent right here:

Permanent Injunctions – Both parties shall be permanently enjoined from the following: Making disparaging, defaming, or discrediting remarks regarding the other party in any manner or medium including published materials, social media posts, social media comments, videos, video messages, text messages, or written correspondence

Communicating directly or indirectly by use of an agent (including by written correspondence, telephone, publication, text message, email, social networking websites or in person) with the other party's business partners, business partners' families, employer, employer's family members, employees, employees' family members, contract workers, contract worker's families, customers, customers' family members, clients, client's family members and the party's friends and friends' spouses and family members of friends.

Both parties agree that they will not register, purchase or use any combination of either party's current or former name or any other name that is representative and is meant to directly or indirectly intended to depict either Ms. Tootsie or Mr. Bauer to secure URLs ending in .biz, .com, .net, .org, or any other publicly available domain for the purpose of financial gain, disparagement, defamation, discreditation, or any other irreparable reputation impact for either party, or for any organization as depicted in Attachment B which is a screen shot of www.herfirstandlastname.com with redirects to the site www. 100shadesofdeception.com.

The parties agree that publishing in any manner any memoir, book, biography or account purporting to depict or discuss the personal relationship, personal details learned during the course of the relationship or personal family matters pertaining to either party including parents, siblings or business partners is strictly prohibited. Such matters include but are not limited to a document that contains the cover art for a purported book that Mr. Bauer purportedly intends to publish depicting a woman's hands wearing the custom engagement ring and wedding band owned (but paid for by Mr. Bauer) by Ms. Tootsie.

The parties agree that comments directed at events involving either Mr. Bauer or Ms. Tootsie or involving any family member of Mr. Bauer or Ms. Tootsie that occurred in the relationship to any person or published in any manner will cause irreparable harm to the other.

The parties agree that they are responsible for their own attorneys' fees, except if enforcement of this agreement is necessary.

Communicating directly or indirectly (including by written correspondence, telephone, publication, text message, email, social networking websites or in person) with the other party's business partners, business partners families, employees, employees' family members, customers, customers family members, and the party's friends and friend's spouses and family members of her friends.

As you can see, they were very eager to have me sign an agreement that would prevent me from publishing anything about the incident. I think they knew this book was coming, and I had them running scared. So what did I have to gain by signing this agreement? Nothing whatsoever. I declined to sign the injunction agreement because legal threats from her lawyers no longer scared me.

During the divorce, I made the mistake of just settling and accepting every agreement I was asked to sign. I didn't press charges, I agreed to let things go, and I left feeling like I had made a huge mistake. Well, I'm not going to make the same mistake twice. I'm not signing anything or agreeing to anything, because I'm now taking control of the situation.

I look back on this relationship and I realize that the biggest red flag that I should have seen is so glaringly obvious now: Relationships should not operate on a tit for tat basis.

Love, true love, is not self-seeking. Love doesn't think, I will give you this if you do this for me. That is how business operates and, yes, it is a part of human nature, but it doesn't have a place in a loving lifelong relationship or healthy marriage.

When you truly love someone and commit to them it doesn't matter what the relationship brings you. You simply want to be with your person. You truly want for them what you want for yourself. You are connected and bonded together.

I truly loved Tootsie and did everything I could for her but my biggest mistake was not seeing what was slapping me in the face. She was in the relationship for what she could get out of it and not me. That is why over and over again I continued to get the feeling that if I just GAVE Tootsie everything that she wanted she would never leave me. I am a confident man, but through her constant seeking of extramarital relationships, this woman kept me teetering on the edge of a cliff of insecurity. I was constantly trying to strengthen my value in the relationship with gifts and romantic gestures when I should have just realized that a woman that truly loved me would never make me question her feelings toward me. I was lost in this relationship, truly manipulated. I've forgiven myself for being blind for those 5 years because, well, Tootsie was very good at deceiving me, and many others. It is so hard to see that you are being manipulated when you are immersed in the middle of it.

However, now that I've taken a step back and have seen how badly I was used, I am much wiser. I have grown so much and because of this growth, I am actually grateful for the entire experience, even though it was incredibly painful to walk through. I get to move on as a better man and I know that I will not let this happen again in another relationship. And speaking of lessons learned...

CHAPTER 11:

LESSONS LEARNED

MY RELATIONSHIP WITH TOOTSIE WAS A FAILURE. BUT the most important thing about failures is what you can learn from them. And in looking back on my relationship with Tootsie, I realize it was never going to last because it lacked all three key ingredients to a real lasting relationship. There are three things I will be looking for in any relationship moving forward. These are going to be non-negotiable for me in all my relationships from here on out. So, if I meet someone great, but our relationship is lacking in one of these ways, sorry, that relationship is over. Better to end it as soon as I realize, rather than dragging it out only to have it fall apart later. I think these are the three things that everyone should be looking for in their relationships because I have figured out the 3 Keys to a FOREVER Lasting Relationship:

A) **AN EMOTIONAL CONNECTION**

This is the most critical part of a romantic relationship. Frankly, if you do not have an emotional connection, I don't even think you can say that you have a romantic relationship. At best, you have a friend that you also like to have sex with. But if you do not have that real emotional connection between you and the other person, you're missing out on the entire romantic relationship between two people.

Given that fact, it's surprising how many relationships DON'T have that emotional connection. But I think it's easy for people to fool themselves into believing it's there. Many people are in love with the very idea of being in love. And who can blame them? Love sounds (and is) wonderful; we see it celebrated in movies and TV, Valentine's Day, and big fancy weddings. Love is something we know is excellent.

But I think people get so obsessed with the idea of being in love. I met a beautiful woman; she was charming and wanted to have sex with me, so I thought I was in love. But we never really had that emotional connection where we spend hours just talking with each other about our deepest thoughts and feelings and opened up to each other. We did at the beginning, but not in the end. Being able to share your soul with another person, that's what an emotional connection is.

It's hard to show that in a TV show or movie, though. So we know what love looks like in a film – there's grand romantic gestures, sex, and a montage of time spent together. It's no wonder that's all we think a relationship is. And you can do those things in your relationship – spend lots of time together, have sex, even throw in the occasional romantic gestures. The relationship needs to be based on emotional connections. If you don't have that, you just have the trappings and appearance of a real connection, but your relationship is hollow inside.

And I think we've all seen those couples who have a hollow relationship. I know, because I was one of them. Two people who are married but don't even seem to like each other. People who can't wait until their husbands or wives go on vacation because they can FINALLY have the house to themselves. Some of these couples break up swiftly; others of them stay together in misery for years.

But if you want a relationship that lasts forever, the one essential thing is an emotional connection. That's what's going to survive after the grand romantic gestures fall off, and the island vacations stop happening, and the sexual attraction fades. Over time, all that other stuff will start to matter less, and you'll either have someone you always want to be with because you feel like you can tell each other anything, or you won't. Emotional connection is the only thing that will have you and the person you marry still gazing at each other with love decades into the future.

B) **BE COMMITTED**

What do I mean by being committed? Commitment is doing what you said you would do, long after the mood and emotion you said in it has left you. It's that simple.

Note that I said it's simple, not that it's easy. Because it certainly isn't always easy to follow through on your word when things change. And things are CONSTANTLY changing.

A few years ago, I had a local friend who needed to get to the airport. Now, it just so happened that I had a conference I was flying out to on the same day as his flight, so I said, "Don't bother arranging a car service, I can give you a ride." I had to drive to the airport anyway, and I knew I could save him a few bucks and give him a more pleasant experience by chatting with him on our way.

But a couple of days before our flight, I get notified that my conference has been postponed. Suddenly, what was going to be no extra trouble for me and only be a net positive, was now going to involve some extra driving on my part in the middle of my day.

Now I had a choice to make. I could have told my friend, "Sorry, my conference got canceled, so you're on your own for getting to the airport." This would not have ruined his life or anything, and he would have had time to hire a car and set up another way to get there. But I had committed to my friend and told him that he could rely on me. If I wanted my word to carry any weight, and to show him that our friendship mattered to me, I could not just rescind my offer to him at the last minute without being a jerk. I decided to honor my commitment, even though my circumstances had changed.

And as often as circumstances change, your mental state changes even more often! How many times have you told yourself something like, "I should reorganize my garage; I will do that tomorrow when I get home from work." And then tomorrow comes around, and work is sort of a long day, and by the time you finally get home, you have absolutely no interest in diving into any new garage projects.

Or you get excited one evening and say, "Hey, I should redesign my website, I haven't updated it in a while, and it could feel a little fresher. I'm going to tackle that first thing tomorrow." And then tomorrow comes around, and there are other things to deal with.

Or you tell yourself, "That's it, I've got to give up on those giant fried blooming onion plates, I know they're not good for me." And then you find yourself out to dinner, and they look pretty good when one arrives at the table next to you, so you end up ordering one anyway.

Our moods and priorities naturally fluctuate. We all tell ourselves we're going to do things and then fail to follow through because we feel differently now than we did yesterday. And that's okay. When you tell yourself you're going to do something, you're allowed to decide not to do it later, because you don't owe anything to the past version of you.

But commitments to others matter. If you tell a friend you'll help them with something when you're feeling full of energy and excited to help, and then the day arrives, and you're just feeling run-down and not enthusiastic, too bad. You made a commitment to another person. If you frequently back out of your obligations, you will not only get a reputation for being unreliable, but you are explicitly showing your friend that they don't matter very much to you.

And of course, this applies tenfold to romantic relationships. If you're considering building a life with someone, you should know that you care about them enough to do for them everything you said you would – even when you don't feel like it. Because no matter how much you love someone, there will always be days when you don't feel like doing anything. But when you genuinely care about someone, you power through and do the thing anyway, because you promised you would, and you know it will make them happy. If you're willing to ignore the commitments you made to your spouse just because you're in a different mood one day, you have to seriously ask yourself whether you're making them a priority. Because if you're not even willing to make this person a priority over a fleeting mood on a random day, why would you try to build your life around them?

By the same token, if you're with someone who isn't committed to you, that's their way of showing you that you are not a priority in their life. If they can't be bothered to keep their commitments to you, they're saying that they don't care about you more than they care about their fleeting day-to-day emotions and moods. I don't know about you, but I certainly wouldn't want to marry someone who couldn't meet that bar. I think for a relationship to last, both people have to be committed to each other.

C) COMMAND A MONOGAMOUS RELATIONSHIP

The last key ingredient I need for a relationship to last forever is to be a monogamous relationship. I know some people don't believe in this anymore. Still, especially after my relationship with Tootsie, I've realized I need this in any relationship I'm going to have going forward.

The biggest reason for monogamy is that I want someone who will devote themselves to me entirely. If we're going to build our life together, I want to know that I am always #1 on their list. They should constantly be thinking of ways to make me happier, and while I would never forbid them from having friends, it needs to be clear to everyone that they are mine. Obviously, at my age, people you're in a relationship with have probably had other relationships before, and that's okay. The important part is that they have no other relationships after because that part of their life is over once they devote themselves to you.

In my relationship with Tootsie, I made the mistake of continually trying to do whatever would make her happy. I paid for everything her heart could desire, and where did it get me? **The problem with putting others first is you have taught them that you come LAST!** When I am in a relationship going forward, I expect to go first on the other person's priority list, all the time. I don't just expect it, I demand it.

I think healthy, lasting relationships have to be monogamous because people's wants and moods continuously change, as we've discussed above. That's the whole point of marriage in the first place: To protect against people's changing moods, and make sure that they stay with the person they married.

Without marriage, people would just go around freely, sleeping with whoever they wanted. I might fall in love with a woman and buy her a car, and tomorrow she might decide she wants to have sex with someone else, and there would be nothing I could do about it. Without marriage, there would be nothing standing in the way of people having sex with whoever they wanted, or moving out to live with whoever else they wanted, no matter how much you had done for them in the past.

Marriage is a way to remove people's other options and say, "Hey, I will provide you these benefits, but in return, you have to promise to be with me." Marriage is a binding legal contract, and just like most binding legal contracts, once you've signed and agreed to it, it's not so easy to just walk away without jumping through a lot of painful and often expensive hoops.

But without monogamy, you're not removing their other options. If your marriage isn't monogamous, you're telling your spouse, "You have to promise to be with me, but you can still sleep with whoever you want." What's the point of making someone promise to be with you if you're then going to let them be with everyone else? Then you're not removing their options at all.

And if you give people lots of options, they might find an option they like better than you. And at that point, the whole thing just falls apart – as I found out the hard way. I might think that I'm a great person to be in a relationship with, but I can never know that someone will always prefer me to every other option. That's why I like to be the only option.

The way I see it, until you get married, you're exploring your options. And that's healthy; everyone should explore their options and try to find the best chance they can. But it's always a gamble because when you see a good opportunity, you never know if that's going to be the best option of your life, or if a better option will come along later. So when I offer someone a relationship, I'm saying, "Hey, I think I'm a pretty good option that comes with lots of benefits, but in return, you have to promise to be done looking at other options." They then get to choose whether to keep gambling or cash out and enter into a relationship with me. And if someone chooses me, then I don't want to give them the option of saying a year later, Hey, I see a better option now, I'm going to do that instead.

I offered Tootsie a relationship when she had no better options, and it's a little unfair that I was her best option then, but suddenly a few years later, she, for no reason, decides she has better options. I brought this on myself by not demanding a monogamous relationship. In exchange for being granted all the benefits of being in a relationship with me, she gave up her other options.

That's a mistake I don't ever plan to make again because I will only be interested in monogamous relationships in the future. For a relationship to truly last forever, through people's mood swings or where they might feel more interested in other people, it needs to be a monogamous relationship. They know that you are #1, and that's the choice they made when they entered into the relationship.

So those are the three keys to a relationship that lasts forever, as I see it. Have an emotional connection, be committed, and have a monogamous relationship. And what helped me realize all of this is necessary for a relationship that lasts forever was seeing how the lack of those three things made my relationship with Tootsie fall apart.

We never had an emotional connection. We had lots of sex, we went on many vacations, I even favored her with grand romantic gestures straight out of the movies, from lavish gifts and fancy dinners to a surprise proposal and a destination wedding. But we never really opened up to each other. Once or twice, I listened to her talk a lot when we were starting to get together. But I didn't ever open up to her, because I didn't feel that connection. We didn't have a lot in common, maybe because she was too young to have developed more personality. We both enjoyed yoga, sex, and the nice things my money could buy. But we never had that more profound emotional connection, so she didn't feel genuinely bonded to me, and was happy to leave.

We never had a genuine commitment. At least, not on both sides. I was committed to always doing everything I could for her, even when it involved spending a considerable amount of time, effort, and money. I ran myself ragged, trying to get her the exact ring I knew her heart desired. But that was all one-sided because she was never really committed to me. She promised she'd take care of me after my major back surgery, and then canceled on me at the last minute and left me out to dry. She had promised when we married to respect me; clearly, she didn't. For that matter, she made promises to her first husband to which she also wasn't committed. I might have been committed to her, but she wasn't committed to me. And a one-sided commitment isn't good enough, because by always putting her first, all I taught her was that I came last. The fact that she wasn't committed to me meant that our relationship wasn't going to last.

And we never had a monogamous relationship. I was never going to be the only man in her life, which was a thing I sort of knew from the beginning, that she was never going to devote her entire life to me. She always kept her options open. We started while she was with her husband, and she kept sleeping with other people throughout our relationship. She got to have lots of sex with whoever she wanted, and eventually, she decided she'd rather be with someone else than me.

<hr>

So that is the complete story of my relationship with Tootsie, from the day we met to the exceedingly bitter end. It seems like another lifetime ago, even though it ended just last year from when I am writing this. I certainly never could have imagined everything that she would put me through, the physical, emotional, and financial pain that she would cause me. I probably lost a quarter of a million dollars in my divorce with Tootsie. How appropriate that this is Chapter 11, right?

That's a business joke. And you might think, "Chuck, this is a story of personal betrayal and romantic relationships, why would you try to make this about business?

Well, two reasons. First of all, that's literally my job. Business is my business. I am always thinking about business; my career has been devoted to helping other people with their business; I can't help but view things from a business perspective. But secondly, and much more importantly, when I think of all the lessons I've learned from this entire ordeal, and the advice I'd want to impart to anyone else reading this, I came to a stunning realization:

I had already learned every single one of these lessons before I ever met Tootsie.

Now, you might well be asking yourself, what kind of damn fool is Chuck Bauer that he says he learned all these lessons before, but then ignored them when it came to his relationship with Tootsie? Well, the answer is simple: I had known these lessons as business lessons but didn't realize that they applied to relationships as well. In fact, every one of these lessons is something that I've been telling my business clients for years.

If I had only realized sooner that I should be applying what I know about business to my romantic relationships, I would have saved myself some serious heartache (and backache, wallet-ache, etc.). It's too late for me to do that for my relationship with Tootsie. But it's not too late for you. I certainly don't want anyone else to have to go through what I went through, especially if they don't have the benefit of my situation where I had many advantages. Thanks to my successful business, it was easy for me to land on my feet when the relationship ended.

So to make sure nobody else makes the same mistakes I did, here are some of the biggest lessons I learned, which I already knew:

1) **You Have To Take Responsibility For Your Own Decisions.**

This is first because it's the most important lesson of all, and the reason the rest of the lessons are essential. Whatever you do is on you. Yes, what happened to me was absolutely a tragedy that I wouldn't wish on anyone. I would never blame myself (or any other domestic violence victim) for being physically assaulted. It's never okay to blame the victim of domestic violence, and if you are a victim of domestic violence, you need to know that it's not your fault.

However, in terms of the broader relationship and how my relationship with Tootsie evolved, all of the things that I did have to be my responsibility. I was the one who chose to start dating her, and I was the one who decided to throw tens of thousands of dollars at her. I was the one who chose to participate in all of her various sexual escapades. She may have asked me or encouraged me, but the decisions I made were all mine, and I have to own that.

I tell this to my business clients all the time: When you're the CEO, the buck stops with you. Whenever a business fails – and a new business fails within the first two years a lot more often than not – the chances are decent that you'll see the CEO try to throw some of the blame anywhere else. You'll hear people talk about how the competition was too well-entrenched to overcome, or how the location just wasn't right, or how the market simply wasn't there.

But the CEO is the one who decided to launch a business with that competition, at that location, in that market. The CEO bears responsibility. That's why I have tremendous respect for any CEO whose business fails and says, "I made some mistakes. I hope to learn from them and do better next time." That's certainly the way I've tried to approach this whole chapter of my life. My relationship with Tootsie included some big mistakes I'll talk more about below, so I'm going to accept responsibility for them, and hope to do better going forward.

This is not everyone's default reaction to failure. You'll see plenty of CEOs caught out doing something illegal, who will try to shift the blame onto an advisor who told them they could get away with it. Or, more recently, with all the dangers of COVID-19 and the lack of sufficient safety precautions in some workplaces, you'll see some CEOs who don't want to take responsibility for the risks of the modern workplace. If people are at risk in the workplace, the CEO is the one who has to answer for it because they decided to accept that much danger instead of taking a safer approach.

You are the CEO of your own life. And that goes double for your romantic relationships. So whatever decisions you make, you will have to live with the consequences. It's too late for me to say, "Gee, I wish I hadn't spent $27,000 buying a custom ring for a woman who wasn't trustworthy," or "I would never have set up all those sex-filled weekends with Tootsie and Wootsie if I knew the two of them were going to run off together." The fact of the matter is, I did do those things, and I have to accept that. I can undoubtedly blame Tootsie for her actions (as I've spent this whole book showing you I do), but I can't blame her for my decisions. These were choices that I made, and the results thereof have reminded me why it's so important to think carefully about my options in the future.

So you are responsible for your own decisions, just like I am. And it's because you are responsible for your own choices, that you should keep the rest of these lessons in mind when making them.

2) Buyer Beware – Due Diligence Is Essential.

This lesson is so old, you've probably even heard it in the original Latin: "Caveat Emptor." Let the buyer beware. When you purchase something, you assume the risks and responsibilities of the product, which is being sold to you as is. And chances are, the person trying to sell it to you is going to embellish all the good points and not mention any of the bad points.

This happens all the time in the business world. A vendor will try to sell you on their miraculous solution that is not only "incredibly easy to use" but will "cut your work in half" thanks to the fact that it's "an extremely versatile system."

And then you hire them and install their system, only to find that it's quite challenging to use, requires more work than what you were doing before to convert things over to their design, and still can't do what you wanted to do. You were sold a bill of goods, believed the hype, and now you pay the price for failing to investigate to find out which of those claims can be backed up.

I've seen people buy a business franchise without really investigating details because it sounds like easy profit to them. They are lured in by the promise of a turnkey operation where everything comes from corporate, and they don't have to worry about things. But of course, as anyone who has ever run a franchise will tell you, there is plenty to worry about. All sorts of issues will crop up, some directly caused by your corporate overlords' restrictions placed on you. Anyone who had investigated would have known this.

That's why buying blindly without due diligence is a terrible idea.

And romantic relationships are no different. Loving blindly without taking the time to do a little due diligence can be a mistake. It certainly was for me. If I had taken the time to investigate and learn more about what kind of person Tootsie was, I probably would have known better than to plan my life around her. But I didn't bother with any of that, because I was in love.

They say love is blind, but that doesn't mean that you have to be. You have to be aware that after the honeymoon phase is over, things may not look as rosy as they did when you first started dating. You have to be mindful that just because someone can turn you on doesn't mean they can't turn on you. There's always a risk, so you should try to be sufficiently aware, so you at least have some idea of what you're getting into.

3) Mitigate Risk – Have a Safety Net In Place

As I said, loving someone is a risk because there's always the chance they could turn on you. When you love someone, it means you become personally invested in them. And from a business perspective, this makes perfect sense; there's no such thing as an investment without risk. But does that mean you shouldn't ever invest, or ever let yourself fall in love?

That would be silly. Of course you shouldn't deny yourself the possibility of the benefits of love, just because there's a risk. And likewise, you'd be missing out on the potential of great returns if you never invested your money in any businesses, stocks, or mutual funds. But what I always tell my business clients is two things: You should try to reduce the risk to yourself as much as possible, and then decide how much risk you are comfortable with.

When it comes to making business decisions, it's easy to get caught up with visions of how much money you'll make if your plans are successful. But the question I always ask clients is, "What's the worst-case scenario here?" Then figure out how to mitigate that. If you're launching a new product, It may be cheaper per unit to produce it at the largest scale possible. But that runs the risk of having a lot of unsold inventory which not only fails to return the money you spent, but ends up costing you money to warehouse. Starting with a smaller production run mitigates risk, and then if it's successful, you can expand as time goes on.

Even with this book, I had the option to print up 50,000 copies at a low per-unit price. But what happens if I only sell 10,000 copies? Suddenly I have 40,000 unsold books and need somewhere to put them. That's why most books start by printing up a more moderate number of copies and then go into second and third printings as necessary, because publishers know that in business, you need to mitigate risk.

That's why insurance exists. Life insurance, home insurance, health insurance, car insurance, all of it is just different ways for us to say, "Gosh, in a worst-case scenario, I could be financially ruined, so let's put a little something in place to mitigate that risk." I hope that my home never burns down in a fire. But if it did, I'd know that because it's insured, I'd be able to find a new place to live and have the money to help do that. It'd still be a tragedy, the emotional impact of losing my home, the giant hassle of having to find a new place to live, and needing to replace my possessions. There would be lots of unpleasantness to go around, but at least I'd know that insurance would give me money to cover a replacement, so I could avoid the worst-case scenario of having my home burn down and being left homeless.

A prenuptial agreement is marriage insurance. You hope that your marriage will never burn down. And whether you have a prenup or not, if your marriage does burn down, there's going to be a tremendous emotional impact. It's going to be a giant hassle, with lots of unpleasantness. But a prenuptial agreement will protect you from the worst-case scenario of having your financial life ruined at the same time that your personal life is being destroyed.

As you know, if you read the rest of this book and didn't just skip right to the last chapter, I suffered a lot when Tootsie suddenly turned on me. When she attacked me, I suffered the physical assault, the emotional trauma of having her leave me, the giant upheaval to my personal life and plans. And all the social issues that our split caused, such as being pushed out of the yoga studio where I had been going for years.

But to add insult to injury, I probably lost $250,000 in the divorce with Tootsie, which was a real shot of financial pain when I had plenty of pain already. And that was an unnecessary hit. If I had just had a prenup, I would have saved $250,000.

I've come to see prenuptial agreements as an absolute necessity for any serious business person considering marriage. Now, some people don't like the idea of a prenup because they say, "if you trust the person, you shouldn't need one," or sometimes, "The very existence of a prenup is insulting and hangs over the marriage.

And I say, that's nonsense. As long as your marriage doesn't break up, the fact that you signed a prenup will end up being entirely irrelevant. If your marriage continues happily, as you hope it does, that prenuptial agreement will not interfere with your marriage in any way. It doesn't make your marriage any less valuable, or something you care less about, just like having home insurance doesn't mean you don't care about taking care of your house.

But even if you trusted yourself to be a great driver, you'd still want car insurance. Even if you exercise every day, you'd still want health insurance. Even if you have every reason to think your marriage should last forever, you should always have marriage insurance, which is how I feel about prenuptial agreements. That doesn't mean you don't trust the other person; it just means you want to mitigate risk.

Now the other thing about risk is that you have to decide if the amount of risk remaining is an amount you can tolerate once you've reduced it as much as possible. And sometimes it's not. Sometimes I'll look at a business proposition and realize that there's no way for me to avoid being completely screwed in a worst-case scenario. And in those cases, sometimes, I will decline an opportunity because I'm just not willing to risk everything. Other times, I will look at my situation and decide, okay, I can take that risk because even if it all goes south, I'll still end up okay.

Deciding how much risk you can tolerate is a personal decision that everyone has to make. And I tell my clients, choosing how much risk you can accept, that's your choice. But mitigating the risk to lower the damage from a worst-case scenario, that's just common sense. And if only I had shown a little of that common sense and shielded myself from the risk of marriage with a prenuptial agreement, I'd be a quarter of a million dollars richer today.

4) People Will Show You Who They Are, So Pay Attention

When I found out that Tootsie was seeing other people behind my back and that she had filed for divorce, I was surprised. But I really shouldn't have been, because the signs were there all along. If I had been paying any attention throughout our relationship, I would have realized that of course that's precisely what would happen. The truth of the matter is: That's who she is.

People don't exist in a vacuum, and their relationship with you is never their only interpersonal relationship. Whatever situations they will share with you are not the only situations they have been in. Whoever you date will have a life and a history that does not include you. So if you want to know what kind of person they are, and what type of behavior you can expect from them, all you have to do is pay attention.

From the moment I started dating Tootsie, I should have known that I couldn't trust her or expect her to be honest. Our relationship began because she had a husband she was unhappy with, rather than telling him and having an open discussion about it. She decided to sneak around with me behind his back. She was with this guy who married her but was always finding herself secretly texting other people and meeting up with them for sex. She and I had already built a life together long before telling her husband she wanted a divorce. That's how our relationship started; I was the "other man."

That's also how our relationship ended, except this time, I was the husband. Other than my change of roles, the story was the same. She was with this guy who married her, but she found herself secretly texting other people and meeting up with them. It seems likely that she had already decided to leave me to be with Wootsie long before she told me that there was a problem or that she wanted a divorce.

Gee, who could have seen that coming?

Imagine if our relationship had started with honesty. Imagine if she had told her husband that she was unhappy with him, and they had talked about it, and she had expressed her desire to sleep with other people. And then maybe her husband refused to let her do that, so she decided to leave him, all before she ever started dating me. If that were the case, then I would have known, here is a woman who respects her husband too much to keep secrets from him.

But what happened was precisely the opposite. I found a woman who I knew full well from the moment we got together, was someone who would keep secrets from her husband. She would cheat behind her husband's back, build a life, plan to exit without telling her husband ANYTHING, and then suddenly abandon her husband with a divorce he never saw coming. And then I signed up to be her husband. Great job, Chuck. She showed me exactly the kind of person she was, and I wasn't paying attention.

The crazy thing is, this is precisely the type of thing I tell people to pay attention to in the business world. I advise anyone running a company, pay attention to the personal character of the people you hire. I even told this to Tootsie's family! You may recall, when Tootsie's uncle asked me for business advice, I gave him my top hiring tip:

When you are down to your final round of interviews and only have a few candidates left that you're deciding between, midway through the last interview with each candidate, you ask the applicant, "What kind of a car did you drive to the interview today?" Then you excuse yourself and tell them you'll be back in a few minutes. Meanwhile, you go out and find the car they mentioned and look at their vehicle. The vehicle directly reflects how the person's cubicle will look (in the most simple terms): a messy car equates to a messy desk.

People don't live in a vacuum, and you can tell a lot about their character by looking at how they interact. This is also why another great tip when making hiring decisions is to take a final candidate out for a business lunch. Watch how they interact with the waiter or the cashier. Anyone rude to the waiter or cashier is someone you don't want working for you. Waiters and cashiers are not in a position of power, so because they can't offer any benefit to your candidate, you get to see how they treat people who can't offer them anything. And I find that very revealing when it comes to character.

Again, that's as true in romantic relationships as it is in business relationships. Someone rude to the waiter or cashier isn't a nice person, and if you ignore that because you want to date them now, it will 100% come back to bite you later. How people act with others is a foolproof guide to how they will eventually act with you. Whether you're deciding whether to hire someone or whether to date them, the most important thing is to look for good people, and it's surprisingly easy to figure out whether people have good character by paying attention to how they behave.

I had an absolute wealth of information about how Tootsie would act. And in every single instance where I chose to ignore it, it came back around, and I suffered for it in the end. I knew from how she treated her ex-husband that she would sneak around behind a husband's back, fall out of love with him while texting others, and have secret affairs before finally and suddenly announcing a divorce that she had been planning for a while. Then she did the same thing to me after I married her, and I became the husband being taken advantage of.

I knew from the whole situation with her father being accused by her aunts of rape that she loved to dive into a problem and play spin doctor, spinning a different story to each person in the audience to control the narrative and keep power over communications. Then she did the same thing to me after the divorce, telling a different story and controlling the narrative among our yoga community, until I ended up feeling like I had to leave the yoga studio where I had gone for years.

I knew from when she had moved in with me and gotten a sham apartment to keep our relationship a secret from her family that she would construct an elaborate lie to present herself a certain way to her family, to the point where they were convinced that she was still in mourning over her divorce when in actuality, she had been shacking up with me for months. We had a life together already in progress. Then she did the same thing when she left me, so her family was convinced I was the bad guy and was in mourning over the divorce when in actuality, she had already been shacking up with Wootsie and had a life with her already in progress.

At every turn, I saw an example of exactly how Tootsie was going to act, but I had written it off as unimportant because she was only hurting other people, and she was still nice to me. That was a huge mistake, and one I have paid the price for. What I should have done was pay attention to how she treated other people and behaved for the rest of her life, and realized that it would be exactly how she would end up behaving with me. Sure, she started off being nice to me because she wanted something, but eventually treated me like she had treated everyone else. In the end, character always comes through.

That's why I like to see how people treat others that can't give them anything; it shows a lot about their character. Which brings up another lesson:

5) True Friends Help You When You're Down.

Again, I tell clients to watch how a potential hire treats cashiers or waiters because those are positions without any power. You can't just see that a potential employee is kind and polite to you and presume that's a sign of good character. It's a sign that the person would like you to think fondly enough of them to pay them money. But when someone is kind to someone with no power, who can't do anything for them, that's when you know you're dealing with someone who has good character.

When you have a successful business, everyone wants to get involved. If you're making money hand over fist or have the next hot property, you will be drowning in partnership offers and people who would be excited to work with you. But if you hit a rough patch, or your offerings just aren't catching on, those partnership offers are suddenly very thin on the ground. And if you do have people willing to invest in you and work with you even when you're not doing well, it's because they believe in you and your business – and those are the type of people you want to surround yourself with.

Similarly, in your personal life, you'll notice that when you're living it up and letting the good times roll, everyone wants to join the party. But when things take a turn for the worse, you'll discover who your real friends are. Tootsie and Wootsie were happy to join me for expensive vacations at lavish resorts, jetting around the Caymans, fine dining, and drinks that never stopped flowing. Who wouldn't be?

But when I had back surgery and needed someone to help me with the recovery, despite both of them having promised to be there, neither of them were anywhere to be found. For me, the people who were there were my sister, her husband, and my good friends, Jennifer, Delinda, and Joe and Sheri. And I'll never forget that. I have plenty of friends who would like to join me in the Caymans, visit my vacation cabanas, or go to fancy restaurants and excellent shows on my dime. But I have very few friends who would volunteer to help take care of me when I'm laid up, and those are the friends I appreciate the most.

It's easy for people to claim to be your friend when you can do something for them. But when your friendship doesn't immediately offer "fringe benefits," it's the people who show up for you anyway that are your real friends. And it's undoubtedly the same in business. Anyone will butter you up if they expect you to pay them money once they're in your good graces. But someone who treats you with respect even when you can't offer them anything is someone honorable.

After Tootsie assaulted me, I also noticed that many of my so-called "friends" in the yoga community stopped talking to me. This was a yoga studio that I thought of as my home away from home for many years, where I got to know a lot of the other regulars and thought we were close. After the assault, most of them stopped talking to me, and very few of them seemed concerned in any way for my well-being. I can think of maybe a half-dozen people who even took the time to check in with me or ask how I was doing with everything. When things are rough, that's when you find out who you can rely on.

This is why I appreciate the National Domestic Violence Hotline. When I was at a real low point in my life, betrayed and assaulted by the woman I loved and desperately needing support, I was able to call them, and they were there to support me. Let me tell you how amazing it was that when I needed someone to be there, this fantastic organization which I wasn't paying anything, who I had no prior arrangement with, who didn't know me at all, made a point of it to be there in my time of need. And for anyone who suffers domestic violence, the Hotline is staffed 24 hours a day, seven days a week, to support survivors whenever they need it. **They accept calls via phone at 1-800-799-7233, by texting LOVEIS to 22522, or online at thehotline.org.**

I don't think I can express how valuable it was to have that kind of unconditional support when I needed it most. But I figured the least I could do was pay it forward, which is why I not only sent them a nice donation once I was back on my feet, but decided to donate 50% of the proceeds from this book to their organization as well, to support the critical work they are doing. If you or your business have a few spare dollars and would like to make a difference, I can tell you that the National Domestic Violence Hotline will use that money to change people's lives for the better by providing much-needed support.

If you take nothing else from this book, I hope you will appreciate that domestic violence is a terrible thing and that victims going through such an awful ordeal benefit from having such an incredible organization to turn to. It's a very worthwhile cause, and I encourage anyone in a position to do so to join me in supporting them, via their website at **thehotline.org**.

6) The Problem With Putting Others First, Is You Have Taught Them That You Come LAST!

There's an old saying in business: "Look out for number one." You have to look out for yourself first, because nobody else is going to. Acting in your own best interests is just common sense, but it's easy to get sidetracked because you want to please others.

That's actually one of the main reasons I got started in my coaching and consulting business. Before I was doing this professionally,

I was working in sales. And while I don't want to boast, I was very good at it. All false modesty aside, I was essentially the best sales-man in the entire organization of the giant international corporation where I was employed. I worked there for five years, and in all that time, I was bringing in more sales than anyone else in the company, to the point where I had placed first in sales figures for 59 of the 60 months I worked there. I was converting referrals into clients, turn-ing former customers into repeat customers, and was generally the most exceptional salesman that this company had ever seen.

What happened next will come as no surprise: People began to ask my advice. Naturally, when you're as successful as I was, people want to take advantage of your expertise. So people would approach me with questions about sales, and I would do my best to answer them. I wanted to help the people approaching me with questions, so I put in the time and effort to give them all the insight I could offer.

Naturally, the result of this was that people came back and asked me more questions and asked me for more advice. And one thing I noticed was that their approach to me began to change over time. When they initially approached me to ask a question, they were always very polite and respectful of my time. They'd say something like, "Hey Chuck, I know you're busy, but I know you're a really great salesman and I was hoping you might be able to help me figure out what I'm doing wrong if you have a few minutes." And when some-one praises you and asks for your advice, the instinctual response we all have is to want to help. And so I did.

But after a few months, the respect for my time seemed to disap-pear. The same people who had once been very polite were now taking me for granted, and sending me messages saying things like, "Hi Chuck, Take a look at this pitch for me. I need it for Friday."

Do you see the difference? It started with people acknowledging the value of my time and asking me if I was willing to spend my valuable time helping them. But after they began to think of my time as rightfully theirs, the politeness began to disappear, and the entitlement started to creep in. They were no longer asking if I had time to look at something, they were telling me to do it. They were no longer thinking about how I might want to spend my time, they were only focused on what they wanted and needed.

And I was encouraging them. Even after the tone of these requests changed from "Please do me this favor if you can spare a few minutes," to "Do this for me, and I need it this way," I continued to do whatever they asked. And because of this, they came to view me not as a fellow human being whose time is valuable, but basically as just another tool and resource that was there for their convenience. As far as they were concerned, Chuck Bauer was simply the name for a machine where they could look up advice, before Google had been invented.

By putting everyone else first, I had taught them that I came LAST. I showed them that I was willing to spend my time answering their sales questions, and it wouldn't cost them anything. I didn't seem to object to the fact that people kept interrupting my day to look at whatever they wanted, so their takeaway was that my time wasn't valuable. I had shown them that their wants were more important than whatever I was doing.

I didn't realize I was doing this, until the US corporate office got word of my exceptional sales figures, and asked if they could make use of my expertise to train their other sales professionals. And that's when it hit me: My expertise has value. And furthermore, my time has value. The corporate office had recognized that what I had to offer was valuable, and so they needed to pay me to receive the benefit of my expertise and my time. Yet here I was giving it away to everyone around me for free!

That's when I started to become a training and sales advisory expert. And as I corrected my mindset, I realized that if I kept going around helping everyone for free, of course they'd keep demanding more and more of my help. People were taking it for granted and viewing me as a disposable tool. But a funny thing happened once I started charging people for my expertise – they appreciated it more and would always thank me for my help. Back when I was answering everyone's questions for free, people would make demands of me and disrespect my time. But now that I was a paid consultant, people recognized the value of my time. They were much more polite to me when they had to pay me than they were when I was doing things for free as a favor!

What I learned from this whole experience is that by constantly putting others first, I was teaching them that I came last. I was so eager to please people that they came to view me as someone whose sole purpose was pleasing them. Obviously, I still help people today, but now I get something out of it. That's why I love being a consultant and a coach – not only because I can charge for my time and expertise, but because it establishes up front that my time is valuable and that my assistance should never be taken for granted.

And did I take this lesson to heart when it came to my personal relationships? Of course not! As soon as I started my relationship with Tootsie, I became "People Pleaser Chuck" all over again. From the first night we talked at the wine bar, I had shown her that she was important and I wasn't, by letting her just talk about her problems for 90 minutes straight while I barely got a word in edgewise. We had started off our relationship by establishing that her problems were more important than whatever I might have wanted to talk about.

As our relationship continued, I continued to put Tootsie's needs first and showed her that my needs came last. I found myself jumping through ridiculous hoops just to make things more convenient for her. There was the time she called me from Seattle and asked me to fly out that evening to spend the night with her, literally arriving at midnight, spending the night, and then flying back at noon in order to avoid her husband who was coming to be with her. She was asking me to spend hundreds of dollars and upend my schedule for two days of travel flying across the country while dodging her husband, all just to satisfy her whim of being with me that night, even though we could much more easily be together any other week.

And I did it, because I was so eager to please her. I thought I was showing her that I truly cared about her and that she should be as invested in our relationship as I was. But what I was actually showing her was that a momentary convenience for her was worth days of my time and however much of my money it cost.

This established a pattern. Whatever she wanted, I made it happen, and it didn't matter how much of my money it cost. I treated her to 5-star dinners and lavish hotels, bringing her on numerous vacations, any one of which would be a once-in-a-lifetime dream getaway for anyone else. But it wasn't long before she began to take that for granted as well, and just expected me to treat her to extravagant vacations as a matter of course.

When she mentioned she wanted a certain ring when we were going to get married, I couldn't find it and could have gotten her something similar. But instead, I had to prove that her whims were more important than my wallet, so I dumped thirty grand on getting the perfect ring customized to her specifications. By the time we were done enhancing it, I'd spent $34,000 on this one ring. Again, I thought I was showing her how much she meant to me. But what I was actually showing her was that she could take advantage of my financial success because my money meant less than her happiness. And take advantage she did.

The most egregious example of this was how I ended up serving as a personal envoy between Tootsie and the women she was trying to sleep with. As I mentioned at the beginning of this chapter, I believe in a monogamous relationship. I want the person I marry to be with me and only me. And I wanted that when I started dating Tootsie as well.

But of course, that wasn't what Tootsie wanted. Tootsie wanted to sleep with other people. And I could have put my foot down and said, "Absolutely not. If we are dating, then you are mine, and you do not get to go out and fool around with anyone else. I don't want you to do that, so if you want to have sex with other people, you can forget about seeing me anymore, because I'm going to dump you." That's what I should have said when she told me she wanted to sleep with other people. But instead, what I said was:

"Okay."

I thought that if I showed her I was willing to put her happiness first, that it would strengthen our relationship. But what it actually did was teach her that my happiness was irrelevant. It didn't matter to her that I didn't like her sleeping with other people, because she wanted it to happen, so that's what was going to happen. And once we had established a pattern of my acceptance, she began to take it for granted that I was fine with her sleeping with other people.

Eventually, she started asking me to approach other people for her. Here I was, someone who didn't want her sleeping with anyone else at all, and now she was expecting me not only to accept it but to actively take part in making it happen. And I did it! I went on Craigslist to arrange multiple people at once for her, and approached women in bars and hotels that she had shown interest in and asked them to sleep with her. I essentially served as a reverse pimp, where I tried to get people to sleep with my woman, and then I paid for it!

All of this happened because I had shown her that she could take me for granted. By constantly putting her needs first from day one, I had taught her that only her needs mattered and that what I wanted didn't matter at all. That's why I say the biggest lesson I learned from all of this is what I said above: The problem with putting others first is that you have taught them that you come last.

YOU CAN BET I WON'T EVER MAKE THAT MISTAKE AGAIN.